INTRODUCTION

Writing your CV or getting ready to do an interview for a job? Chances are you have lots of questions. *Should I? What if? How can I? Help!* This book gives highly practical and instantly actionable advice on 101 issues, questions and scenarios most frequently encountered by people when applying and interviewing for jobs. When you don't have your own personal CV and interview coach on speed dial this book is the next best thing . . . and costs a lot less. Straight-talking, instructive and using templates and worksheets to help you give the employer exactly what they want to see and hear, it will make the task of securing your ideal job significantly easier and a lot less stressful.

Sinéad English is a career consultant and highly engaging speaker across all aspects of managing your career. She has helped thousands of clients secure their ideal job by advising on how to write CVs that get noticed and preparing them to deliver excellent interview performances. She set up the career advisory firm Hilt in 2007. Learn more at www.wearehilt.com

For John, Emmet, Aoibhinn and Hugh

CV & INTERVIEW 101

HOW TO APPLY AND INTERVIEW FOR JOBS

SINÉAD ENGLISH

POLARIS
PUBLISHING

This edition first published in 2019 by

POLARIS PUBLISHING LTD
c/o Aberdein Considine
2nd Floor, Elder House
Multrees Walk
Edinburgh, EH1 3DX

www.polarispublishing.com

Distributed by Birlinn Limited

2

ISBN: 978-0-9575076-4-7
eBook ISBN: 978-0-9575076-5-4

British Library Cataloguing-in-Publication Data
A catalogue record for this book is available on request from the British Library.

Designed and typeset by Polaris Publishing, Edinburgh

Printed in Great Britain by MBM Print SCS Limited, East Kilbride

YOUR CV

1

What is your CV's job?

Your CV has only one job to do: get you an interview or put you on a shortlist that moves you to the next stage of the selection process.

Your CV should tell the employer that you have experience and achievements that *could* be of benefit to them. The words you use throughout the CV should give them evidence that you can meet the requirements and challenges of the job and make a great contribution to their company.

If a real-live human being is the first to review it (increasingly unlikely) a good CV will make them sufficiently interested, curious or just downright fascinated to meet you. They will want to ask you questions about what they have read. If the CV is analysed by a robot searching for keywords (quite likely) your CV needs to give them enough fodder to tip you into the *Yes* list. Once your CV has done that it can relax and take a break – mission accomplished. Then it's over to you in the interview to bring the words on the CV to life.

2

CV vs LinkedIn

'I don't need a CV anymore. I have a LinkedIn profile – surely that'll do the trick.' WRONG. Some employers advertising jobs on this social networking platform will invite you to apply using your LinkedIn profile. One click and off goes the application. What could be easier? This will work well under certain circumstances.

1. You are 100% sure that your profile is excellent.
2. You are applying for a role that closely matches your past work experience – it's all about the keywords and ensuring the skills you have listed on your profile match what the job advert is looking for.

Here's the problem with this one-click-and-you're-done approach: we have seen thousands of LinkedIn profiles and most of them are far from excellent. 49% of profiles on the platform are incomplete. You could be sending a half-baked profile to the employer for a job you would love to get – good luck with that approach.

Even when a job advert invites you to apply using your profile, most employers will also give you the option to attach a CV. If you are to maximise your chances of getting an interview this is not an option – you *need* to do this.

3

Applicant Tracking Systems – ATS

So much for *Human* Resources. Do humans even look at CVs anymore – or is it all robots?

If you click an 'Apply Now' button to apply for a job it's almost certain that your CV is going to be run through an ATS. Here's a scary statistic – over 75% of CVs are rejected by the ATS without ever being seen by a human. When you receive an automated 'Thank you for your application but you have been unsuccessful . . . ' email you would really like to think that someone, ANYONE took the time to diligently review and consider your CV before they sent you that email. They didn't. The robot did it.

Four ways to maximise your chances of getting past the ATS

• Keywords are everything. This is all the ATS has to assess when it is analysing your CV. Mirror the exact words they used in the job description. Match the language and terminology they use. Think of it as an exercise in the card matching game snap. If they want it, make it crystal clear that you have it. ATS robots can't interpret that the 'several accounting software packages' you mentioned you worked with are in fact Sage and Quickbooks. It will think that you don't have that experience and you will probably end up in the *No* pile.

• Avoid tables, charts, graphics and logos. You may think they look slick but the ATS will churn out a rejection as it won't be able to interpret what is in the tables or depicted on those amazing charts you spent hours perfecting. Keep it simple. Clear section headings, plain bullet points, no fancy fonts, borders or shading. Go easy on the boxes, tables and formatting. Content that is highly stylised and uses data visualisation or snazzy infographics to explain what you are offering (think pie charts indicating how much time you have spent in each job or bar charts depicting your level of proficiency in particular skills) is also a tough one for the ATS to figure out.

• Keywords are good but resist the temptation to go overboard. Mentioning the same keyword two or three times throughout the CV is enough to make an impact. You are not the first person to think it is a great idea to put multiple keywords in white ink in the footer of the page. Invisible to the human eye but the ATS will pick them up. Genius! *Wrong*! The ATS will flag blatant keyword stuffing and your plan will backfire.

• And speaking of headers and footers – many of the CVs we see have the name and contact details of the candidate neatly displayed in a header or footer on the document. The problem with this is that some ATS cannot read these sections. There are enough potential reasons why you may not be contacted for an interview – don't let the fact that the ATS couldn't figure out who you are or how to contact you be one of them!

4

OK, enough about robots . . .

Back to the humans. How long will they take to review my CV?

On a good day employers will take a maximum of thirty seconds to review the CV and decide if they are interested enough to read on. Some research puts this figure as low as six seconds.

*What? It's taken me **two weeks** to write my CV. It's a masterpiece. Are you seriously telling me that if a human being reads it they will give it an average of six seconds before they decide to bin it or interview me? What can they possibly find out in that time?*

Plenty, as it happens. They are checking if it passes the Glance Test. Sloppy formatting, unclear section headings, important information that provides evidence of the required experience or skills being buried deep on page two, spelling mistakes and 'personal profiles' lifted straight from a Google search are the main reasons why CVs will get rejected so quickly. Get the basics right and they will keep reading.

5

Don't state the obvious
– we know what it is

We know it's a Curriculum Vitae so you don't need to put 'Curriculum Vitae' at the top of the document. Put your name in the centre in a font that is at least 4 points larger than the font used in the body of the CV. And never be tempted to put a black frame around the perimeter of each page. It's depressing and makes us want to ask who died. There are still a few free CV templates floating around the internet that have this as standard. Unfortunately, we haven't managed to eradicate all of them yet.

6

Does anyone print CVs anymore?

Hard copy? Hardly ever. Over 90% of employers want your CV emailed or attached to a form on their application website. There are a few exceptions. Hard copy versions will work for local small businesses where you can go door-to-door distributing your nicely printed CVs. Some employers at career fairs or career expos may also take a hard copy (but would really prefer if you emailed it to them or submitted it via their ATS so their robots can give it a good three-second interrogation).

And in case you're thinking, 'I'll print it out on nice thick paper. Best quality, might even go for a nice shade of blush rather than white – that'll make them notice me,' don't bother. You will have the employer thinking style over substance before they even start looking at the content. Avoid.

7

How long is too long?

The rules on this are pretty clear. For 95% of people, a CV should be **NO MORE THAN** two pages. And just for clarity, and to prove that your reasons for why you think you should be in the 5% exception zone don't stack up, here is a list of all of the types of jobs/professions that can get away with their CV being longer than two pages:

- Academics
- Medical doctors

That's it.

And yes, we hear this all the time. 'But I've had such a varied career – twenty-five-plus years and counting of experience. It's just impossible for me to fit it onto two pages.' It *is* possible and to have a good shot at getting called for an interview you have to do it. We had a client who came to us with a thirteen-page CV – font size 8.5. They claimed that everything on there was hugely relevant and nothing could be taken off. They genuinely couldn't figure out why the hell they were not getting interviews – they had great experience. We got the CV to two focused pages and they got the interview. Every two or three years they came back to us asking us to update it as they were applying for a new role. And every time they sent us the CV to update it had somehow, magically, expanded to six-plus pages again. They were addicted to adding CV content and our job was to hack it back again to maximise their chances of getting an interview.

8

What's in a name?

You've emailed in your CV. What name did you give the document? Tell us it wasn't CV.docx or MyCV.pdf . . . Can you imagine how many documents of that name get sent to hiring companies each week? Call the document YourName_CV. For example, JaneJones_CV.docx or AlexJones_CV.pdf. Don't try to be hilarious with the name of the CV you save onto your laptop. We know someone who, rather unwisely, saved and sent their CV called MoneyMoney.docx to a company. Guess what the first question they were asked in the interview was – much to the amusement of the interviewer and downright horror of the candidate?

9

What email address to use?

We are always amazed at how many people use their existing work email addresses when actively looking for a job outside their current workplace. Unless you want your boss to know you are planning to leave (maybe a negotiation tactic?) use another personal email address that is not owned by your employer. Also, don't scare them off before they've even started to read your CV by having an email address that makes you sound like a lunatic. Applying for a role in a financial institution and using the email address sadblacktears@XXX on the CV is not a great move. (True story, we had a client who did this – no one wanted to meet them.)

10

Postal address on my CV?
Do I have a choice?

Employers rarely send letters in the post anymore. Putting addresses on CVs has been shown to potentially introduce elements of negative bias into the selection process. '*They live there? Too far away. They will never make it to work on time.*' Or '*They live THERE? Terrible part of town. Next CV please.*' It happens. Don't include your postal address unless they specifically ask you for it or you can use it to give yourself a tactical advantage – e.g. you are applying for a job as a teacher in the school that is very close to where you live. Showing them that you are a 'local' will play to your advantage, so use it.

11

What font works best?

Here's a quick font tutorial. There are two types (geddit?). Serif fonts, and ones without the Serif – which are called Sans Serif (and you thought you would never use your school French again). Serif fonts have small finishing strokes at the end of each character, while Sans Serif fonts do not. People who know a lot about typography maintain that the cleaner Sans Serif fonts give better readability to your CV. Which is interesting because a large percentage of CVs are still written in the grand dame of Serif fonts – Times New Roman.

Let's put things in perspective. There is no need to get too twisted up about debating the difference between Cambria or Tahoma. And we're *pretty* sure a CV is not going to be rejected for choosing a tried and tested Times New Roman font. Here are a list of recommended fonts to use on your CV. Any one of these will give you a professional-looking CV. But don't mix your fonts. Select one and use it consistently throughout the CV. Nothing says 'I have used a ridiculous amount of cutting and pasting to put this CV together' than a rag-bag of fonts.

Rule of thumb – if you think the font looks decorative or stylish you've probably gone too far. And step away from the jovial **Comic Sans**.

Sans Serif Fonts	Serif Fonts
Verdana	Garamond
Tahoma	Cambria
Arial	Georgia
Trebuchet MS	Times New Roman
Calibri	
Helvetica	

Size of font

Use a 12-point font size on the main body of text on the CV. If you are struggling to fit everything on two pages you could go to 11 or 10.5 point. If you're getting desperate, 10 is just on the edge of acceptable. Anything less than 10 is going to be challenging to read and won't help your case. If you are using 12 for the main text then you could use 13 on the section headings and 16 for your name at the top of the CV. If you are starting your career or don't have much content for the CV, don't be tempted to use a supersized font just to fill up the space. That will look ridiculous.

12

Typos – I have an excellant attention to detail

Do we even need to talk about typos? Let's be realistic. Contrary to popular belief, if you have experience or a skillset that is in demand, employers are probably not going to bin your CV if they spot one . . . or even two commonly made typos. And if you are in that category – good for you. But for everyone else who is navigating the competitive job market where there are more qualified candidates than jobs available – you'll need to adopt your best forensic CSI approach when proofreading your CV. Or better still – you've been looking at it for far too long. Hand it to someone who is looking at it with fresh eyes. Chances are they will find a typo.

Spellcheck is not your friend. A company trying to sell us a service sent an email recently which started

Dear Sinned . . .

Spellchecker had helpfully changed Sinead to Sinned – and they hadn't noticed – until the email had been sent.

13

Truths, near-truths and mis-statements

Of course, I am not going to LIE on my CV. But . . . is an *elaboration* of the truth OK? When is it ok to s-t-r-e-t-c-h the truth, and by how much? In a survey published in the UK in 2017[1] over 5,000 CVs were analysed to determine if they contained false information. 80% of those examined contained one or more discrepancy. If your CV has a few fibs in it you're in good company. What do people lie about on their CVs? Here are the main culprits.

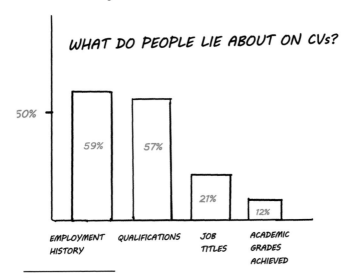

WHAT DO PEOPLE LIE ABOUT ON CVs?

59%	57%	21%	12%
EMPLOYMENT HISTORY	QUALIFICATIONS	JOB TITLES	ACADEMIC GRADES ACHIEVED

---

[1] The Risk Advisory Group, CV Lies 2017

But there are lies and there are LIES and they have different outcomes if discovered. Stating that you were a key member of a team that delivered a large IT project for Zippy IT Solutions when in reality you were drafted in three-quarters of the way through the project as a junior team member is in the category of *stretching the truth*. You had better be ready to explain that project in detail if you get an interview.

Stating that you worked for Zippy IT Solutions for two years when you just interned there for three months is clearly in the category of *downright lie*. This one will obliterate your chances of getting the job if and when they uncover it.

Most serious for employers – and for you – are lies on your CV about your **work experience** (i.e. names of employers and dates of employment) or your **qualifications** (levels, grades and where the qualifications are from). It's fairly easy for employers to check the facts about these. It's not surprising that there is a much lower rate of lying about experience and education in LinkedIn profiles – it's too easy to get caught out.

If employers find out that you have been lying, or even stretching the truth, about key areas of your work experience or education your place on their *Yes* list will start to look shaky and you are quite likely to be kicked off the list entirely. And if you absolutely feel the need to spice up your CV with a few fibs, employers are much less concerned about the lies you tell when you describe how you like to jog, cycle and cook in your spare time. Minimise the impact of being rumbled and put all your lies and wild exaggerations in here. *Attend the gym regularly? Why, of course I do.*

14

Chronological and functional CVs – what's the difference?

A CV written in the **chronological** format will list and give a description of each job you have held starting with your current or most recent job and working back to your oldest job. Most CVs are written this way and employers expect and prefer this format. So what is a **functional** CV and why would you bother with it if employers clearly prefer the chronological format?

A functional CV presents an overview of the skills, accomplishments and experience you have gained over your entire career. It uses section headings like 'Relevant Skills' and 'Career Achievements' to list the qualities and experience you have that are relevant to the role. These sections will include a combination of evidence gathered from several different jobs you have done over the years. It may have a very brief section with **dates** listed for each job you have done but the time you have spent at each job may not always be obvious in a functional CV. A functional CV is a useful way to disguise or de-emphasise gaps in your employment, the fact that you have had five jobs in the last two years or that you have little relevant work experience. Its ability to muddy the waters is why many employers' first thought when they see one is, '*Okay, what are they trying to hide here?*' Avoid.

15

CV Sections – what comes first?

Great. You're ready to start writing your CV. What section should be first? Work Experience, Education, Skills . . .? Research it and you will find conflicting advice at every turn. Cue confusion. We're here to help. Drumroll for our failsafe advice . . .

It Depends

There is only one rule when thinking about how to order and present the information on your CV. **Lead with your best cards**. Get to the good stuff – fast.

If the information that is most relevant to you being able to do the job is halfway down page two, chances are they will never get to it. They will have lost interest after six seconds of trying to figure out why you have even applied for the job. You need to get them interested in you as quickly as possible.

We have outlined three sets of **career circumstances** we see most frequently when working with clients. To help you structure your CV, and lead with your best cards, we have outlined a suggested CV roadmap for each scenario.

Candidate 1. Several years' work experience. Applying for a new role in the industry they are currently working in.

Section 1: Bullet point summary
- 3-4 bullet points summarising your relevance to the role
- A bullet point is no more than 2 lines!

Section 2: Key skills and expertise
- Get the keyword count up
- Use columns of text when listing skills to maximise space

Section 3: Work Experience – could also be called Career Experience or Professional Experience
- Dynamic description of what you do/have done
- Repeat keywords and focus on achievements, not a boring job description of 'duties'

Section 4: Education and Training
- Emphasise continuing professional development
- But don't include every single short course you've ever done – be selective

Candidate 2. Several years' work experience in one industry. Retrained to change industry and/or career direction. Now applying for a role in this new industry for which they have minimal or no work experience.

Section 1: Bullet point summary
• 3-4 bullet points
• Mention the new training/education you have completed so that the employers can quickly see your relevance to the role

Section 2: Recent Education
• Summary of what you have studied
• Include course content to increase keyword count
• Include brief summary of projects completed that have most relevance to the role

Section 3: Relevant Work Experience (if you have any)
• Even though you may not have spent much time here give it prominence on the CV. Sell it!

Section 4: Other Work Experience
• While the content of what you did may not be relevant to the new role you are applying for, focus on what you achieved and the skills you showed

Section 5: Other Education and Training
• Include details of other qualifications
• All education and training is good. It just doesn't all need to be on Page 1 of the CV if it's not relevant to the new role you are applying for now

Candidate 3. Recent graduate or school leaver. Some work experience in typical 'student job' roles but minimal or no relevant work experience.

Section 1: Bullet point summary

3 points summarising:
- Your Education
- Your Work Experience and the skills you demonstrated throughout it
- Your Career Aim

Section 2: Education

- Employers are 'buying' this as you probably don't have much relevant work experience
- Summarise course content and mention relevant modules – remember keywords
- Don't list every module you have ever done – be selective
- Projects can be a proxy for the relevant work experience you may not yet have – give a summary of two projects
- Mention overall grade achieved – if it's good!

Section 3: Work Experience

- If you have completed a placement as part of your course or have any experience relevant to the role mention this first – even if you have **more recent** non-relevant work experience.

Section 4: Interests and Achievements

- This is your chance to differentiate yourself from all the other hundreds of students on your course. See 29

16

The Bullet Point Summary

Employers hate generic rubbish on a CV. One of the quickest ways to get your CV rejected is to put a summary at the top and stuff it with a large selection of meaningless superlatives in an effort to describe yourself. This is a complete waste of valuable CV space and has the employer reaching for the delete button. If your profile cannot pass the 'Best Friend Test' it needs to be scrapped and rewritten.

Best Friend Test:

Take five CV summaries/personal profiles, one of which is yours. Line them up and show them to your best friend or someone who knows you very well. Can they immediately identify which is your one? At a minimum – and remembering the importance of keywords – it should mention your past employers, job titles, length of career experience and relevant education. **And it needs to do that in no more than six lines**. If your best friend is struggling to pick you out of the line-up because you (along with just about everyone else) have described yourself as a '*dynamic, target driven individual with excellent problem solving skills*' (sound familiar?) then you need to fix it.

A generic profile constructed with a collection of CV 'power words' nicked from Google is worse than none at all.

Here are two summaries both describing the same person. If you were an employer hiring for a medical devices sales role, which candidate would you be interested in?

Summary A

- Highly motivated and dynamic sales professional with a significant experience of providing excellent customer service.
- Reliable with excellent attention to detail and the ability to work under pressure to meet deadlines and targets.
- Used to working independently under own initiative but equally effective in contributing to teams.

Verdict: Generic waffle and completely uninformative – employer will have no idea if the candidate has the experience and qualifications they need.

Summary B

- Sales professional with over ten years' experience in managing and building sales relationships in the medical devices sector when working for Livelong Ltd and HealthPlus Inc.
- Achieved an average of 10% over target for annual sales revenues for the last five years.
- Holds BSc in Biomedical Engineering and a Diploma in Business Management from ABC university.

Verdict: Focused, quantifiable, informative and encourages you to keep reading the CV to find out more.

Candidate B will get the call for an interview – every time.

17

Do I need a completely different version of my CV for each job application?

No. But each CV may change slightly to target exactly what they are looking for in the job description. The most effective and time efficient way to do this is to **change your bullet point summary** – not rewrite the whole CV. Reflect the language of the job description when summarising your experience. Remember keywords and the fact that they are scanning the CV very quickly and looking for how you meet the criteria. If the job description mentions that one of the key requirements of the role is to 'develop and implement processes and systems to ensure efficient operation of the department' then, in the bullet point summary, tell them that you have experience of doing that. For example:

• *Five years' experience **of developing and implementing processes and systems** to maximise the **efficiency** of the procurement process of MegaBuys plc.*

They can then quickly see your immediate and direct relevance to the role.

18

Work Experience – ~~Duties include~~ . . .

Stop! Do not put the words 'Duties' or 'Responsibilities' as a heading on this section.

Resist the temptation to transfer the text of your current or previous job description and use it on your CV to describe that job. A job description is just a list of duties and responsibilities and gives very little evidence of **how well** you did them or what you achieved. Put some value-added into it.

We have seen several CVs whose owners have just cut and pasted the content of old job adverts to describe what they did in their past and current roles. Some of them didn't even go to the trouble of changing the font between one cut and paste job and the next. And they can't figure out why they are being rejected. The employer just sees a shopping list of tasks and has no idea how well you did them. You haven't given them enough evidence that you can successfully do what's required.

19

Employers love data

When describing your Work Experience, give them as many numbers and data points as you can. Data provides proof that you have achieved and succeeded. A few well-placed numbers will give evidence of your ability much more effectively than lines and lines of wordy bullet points.

Here's what we mean . . .

• Lead the firm's highest performing team of **16** accounting technicians in **4 locations** across Europe.
• Key point of contact for the firm's relationship with **10 clients** each generating annual client revenues of **£1.5 million.**

Or you can can bore them with a set of vague claims which offer no proof that you actually succeeded at all.

• Lead a team responsible for dealing with client account queries.
• Senior contact for several large client relationships.

20

Describing your Work Experience. Competencies are key

Rather than listing the tasks and responsibilities of your job, tell them **what competency you demonstrated** by completing these tasks. Take the scenario below and examine which CV, A or B, does a better job of explaining the role.

You are describing your role as an accountant. Which CV entry, **A or B**, will appeal more to employers?

A) Jan 2019-Present   Tax Accountant
                                 Fiscal & Co

- Prepare monthly and annual financial reports
- Calculate tax liabilities and complete statutory tax returns

B) Jan 2019-Present   Tax Accountant
                                 Fiscal & Co

- Work accurately to **extremely tight deadlines** when preparing the monthly and annual financial reports and returns for the company's Managing Director.

• Demonstrate detailed knowledge of tax law and **lead client teams** for 10 key clients to advise on minimising their statutory tax liability

B shows the employer how you **exhibited the competencies** they are looking for. **A** just lists what you did. **B** gets the interview.

Scenario 2 – you have no relevant work experience – we are firmly in the CV equivalent of silk purse, sow's ear territory

You have just finished university or school and you are targeting a marketing job. You've had plenty of part-time jobs but have no relevant work experience in the area you want to work in. How can you make your work experience appear relevant on the CV?

Let's face it. The hotshot marketing company are not going to be wowed by the fact that you cleaned the floor, put out the rubbish and locked up the premises at the end of each evening when you worked in a bar. Instead, tell them about the **competencies** you showed while doing it. Chances are while working in the bar you demonstrated that you could:

• Work under pressure
• Deal with challenging clients/customers
• Show adaptability to quickly changing circumstances
• Make decisions and solve problems

All of these competencies are entirely relevant to a role in marketing and probably all appear on the job description. Weave these competencies into your description of your work experience and it will be much easier for them to see your relevance to the role. You will also increase your keyword count for the ATS.

21

How many ways can I say . . . customer service?

'I've had four jobs with four different employers but I've done the same thing in each job. How can I make them all sound different?'

Trying to find four different ways to say exactly the same thing is pretty torturous and will look contrived. Don't bother. Instead, give one job title and list the dates and four employers on lines one under the other – see opposite. Then give ONE extensive description of what you did in these four roles. If you want to expand on this, you could also select one project/initiative that you delivered for each role and give a short description of that.

We have seen some CVs where the candidate listed each of the similar jobs separately and then used exactly the same text (cut and paste) to describe each job. They couldn't even be bothered to try to think of different ways to describe the jobs. Maybe they were trying to be strategic and were thinking of their keyword count? We doubt it. Reading the same paragraph four times won't impress the ATS and definitely won't impress a human.

2007-2018	**Retail Sales Assistant –**
	Technology & Multimedia

2014-2018	BuyMoreStuff Ltd
2011-2013	BestPrices Ltd
2008-2010	Tech & Gadget Store
2005-2007	Phones4You

• Then include one description summarising what you did and achieved in all four roles.

• Make sure to mention if you were given more responsibility as you moved from one role to the next.

22

I've had six different employers in three years – do I look like a flake?

Quite possibly. You will need to explain yourself. If your CV shows that you were in a job for less for 12-15 months, you can be sure that anyone reviewing it will be wondering why. Don't have them thinking the worst. Give them some context in the CV about why you moved from one job to the next. Avoid deferring to the standard **Reason for Leaving** line we often see routinely inserted at the end of each job description – BORING.

- If your jobs were short-term contracts (or even long-term contracts that ended sooner that you expected) put (*Contract*) after the job title. It's not unusual to have a number of contract roles over the course of a few years. Your six employers in three years are not now a cause for concern – that's the life of a contractor.
- Avoid mentioning months – just state the year if you were in a job for less than 12 months and then spent the rest of that year looking for your next job.
- If the company closed, merged, or your job was eliminated due to circumstances outside of your control then you should mention that at the end of your description of the role. For example: 'Engineering

division was closed following the merger of Techteam with Techtrain.'

• If you joined a company and left it within two months or weeks (!) when you realised the job was not what you had expected or because **you were fired**, our advice would be to try to avoid putting that job on your CV at all. Let's be clear here: it's *your* CV. You can choose what goes on it and what doesn't. And chances are if you were in a job for less than two months you probably don't have a whole lot you can say about what you did or achieved there. When addressing a very short stay in a role, finding the balance between presenting what you have in the best possible light and lying can be challenging. Make a determination on whether or not you think the short role was significant or not to your overall career story and include or omit it accordingly.

• If you are applying for a role that requires police or security clearance you will have less scope (i.e. none) for choosing to omit roles. You will be asked to list every job you have held. Similarly, for online application forms, when they say 'list every role' they mean EVERY role. Omitting one (even a really short one) is tantamount to lying – see 13.

23

Mind the gap.
How to explain it.

Employers don't like unexplained CV gaps. They become instantly suspicious of what you may have been doing. Don't give them any reason to think the worst.

> Scenario 1: You have taken time out of the workplace to **take care of family members**

Then just say that. State the years – from 20XX to 20XY and call it what it is:

2007–2016   Career break to care for family

No need to try to justify yourself by adding some dynamic description of how you spent those years juggling cooking, cleaning and ferrying the kids to fifteen activities per week, which clearly shows your ability to work under pressure and manage multiple tasks. Employers KNOW what's involved. Just state the years so that they can account for the time. That's all.

Can you account for some part of the gap by mentioning a course you completed during that time in the CV's Education section? Use years rather than months to describe how long the course was. If the gap was three years from 2016-2018 and you spent four months in 2017 completing a training course, then use the year rather than the months to describe the dates for the course.

2017   Certificate in Office Administration   AllTech College

Have you done any unpaid volunteering work while unemployed and looking for work? You can include that in the Employment section. Just because you didn't get paid doesn't mean it wasn't contributing to your Work Experience – use it to help plug the gap.

Still looking at an empty block of time on the CV? You could use the phrase *Actively searching for employment* to fill in a gap of up to one year. Unwise to claim that you were **actively searching** for more than one year – makes them wonder why you couldn't find a job with all that activity going on.

Sign up to do a training course. There are thousands of free courses available to jobseekers to help retrain and obtain new skills required by employers. Demonstrating to employers that you are committing to additional learning and training will be seen positively. Take advantage of the courses available and plug the CV gap in the process.

24

I took a year out of the workplace to travel the world. How do I explain that on my CV?

The first thing to consider is that most employers will look at that on your CV and think to themselves, 'I wish I had done that.' Without going over the top trying to make your travel adventures sound like a year-long corporate team-building exercise, give a few highlights of what you did while travelling. Link them to competencies sought by employers. For example:

• While in Tanzania volunteered with a local community group and assisted the group leaders with sports activities for schoolchildren.
• Planned the route and travelled independently across Ecuador and Peru for two months.
• Posted a travel blog on social media and gained 1,000 followers by the end of the year.

25

I've run my own business for years. I've never needed to write a CV — until now. How do I start?

Although you didn't need a CV, you still had a job. You were the employer. Describe what you did and what you achieved. Use the template for Candidate 1 or Candidate 2 – see 15.

26

Describing your Education

How much space on the CV to give this depends on what you are selling to the employer. If you have lots of relevant work experience and it's been a long time since you completed your education then you are primarily selling your work experience in the CV. Focus on the content in the Work Experience section. In the Education section it's enough to just state the name of the qualification, awarding body and the year. If it's more than fifteen years since you completed your second level (school) education then don't mention the year. Keep them guessing to minimise the likelihood of age discrimination and maximise your chances of getting an interview.

But what if you have no relevant work experience and the only thing that is making you relevant to the role you're applying for is the fact that you are in the process of completing your degree in Food Science and Technology? If you are a student applying for a graduate job and all you have to offer is your degree results, then it's back to what we said about playing your best cards. You need to make yourself relevant to the job and your education is currently the only way to do that – so use it. Mention modules, summarise projects and talk their language when describing what you learned in your degree.

27

I started but never finished my degree / diploma / certificate. Should I mention it on the CV?

Don't be vague about it and hope they won't check. If you put the name of the qualification on the CV then it's reasonable for them to assume that you have completed it.

Nothing says 'thanks but no thanks' faster than lying or being deliberately misleading about your qualifications. Ask Scott Thompson[1].

If you didn't complete the course – then tell them that. You won't be the only one. Depending on the subject and college, non-completion rates for third level courses can be as high as 50%. If you completed one year of a three-year degree then state:

2018-2019 Bachelor of Business Studies, Apollo University
Completed Year 1 of 3 year course.
Modules completed in Year 1 included: Financial Information Analysis and Corporate Finance.

There is no need to give them a long (or any) explanation on the CV of WHY you did only one year. Just have a great answer ready for that question when you are in the interview.

---

[1] In 2012, Scott Thompson, ex-CEO of Yahoo Inc. announced he was 'leaving the company' when it was discovered that he had stated on his bio that he had a Bachelor's degree in Accounting and Computer Science when, in fact, the degree was an Accounting degree only.

28

How many is too many?
Education course overload

'I like to keep my skills up to date and have done lots of Continuing Professional Development (CPD) training courses – shall I list all of them on the CV?'

No! Be selective. We see some CVs where a full page has been dedicated to a list of completed training courses – everything from four-year degrees to one-hour webinars make an appearance and are given equal billing. The training most relevant to the role is probably in that list somewhere but most employers won't be bothered to wade through it to find them. If a one-hour online course on *Introduction to Project Management* is all you have, then go for it and put it in the Education and Training section, but if you have plenty to choose from then be smart about how you present the information.

If you have done a lot of training, consider dividing them into two section headings to make it easier for the employer to find the information.

Education and Qualifications
Include formal training where you gained a qualification or certification – e.g. PhD, Degree, Certificate, Diploma.

Other Training

Mention work-based training you have done (usually courses of between one hour and three days in duration). Focus on the ones that are **relevant to the job** you are applying for (not every course you've ever done and definitely not hobby and leisure time courses). Examples would be *Manual Handling*, *Introduction to Anti-Money Laundering, Effects of GDPR, Workplace First Aid* . . .

Attending your weekly *Creative Bookbinding* night class might be the highlight of your week but it's not going to add much to your CV when applying for a job in just about every other industry.

29

Should I put Hobbies and Interests on my CV? Does anyone care?

The more work experience you have the less important this section becomes. Once you have clocked up seven-plus years of work experience it should be deleted from the CV.

Mentioning what you like to do in your spare time will be of interest to employers if you are starting out in your career, a recent graduate, or re-entering the workforce after a break. Use it to help employers get a better sense of what makes you tick when there isn't much evidence of relevant work experience on the CV. Call this section **Interests and Achievements** (never use the word *Hobbies* – they *really* don't care about those). The well-used line about enjoying walking, reading and swimming isn't going to have them itching with curiosity to meet you. Make your engagement with them sound dynamic and useful. How about:

Walking: founding member of local community walking group which has increased members to 150 since starting two years ago

Reading: member of local book club and regularly arrange for local authors to give talks to the group

You get the idea.

However . . . if you have lots of experience and are applying for mid to senior level roles **no one cares** what you are interested in or what you like to do in your spare time. Don't waste valuable CV space telling them.

30

Referees – should I mention them?

For anyone **except** recent graduates or career starters, employers do not need details of referees on your CV. They are not going to contact them until after they have interviewed you. They can ask you for the referee details at that stage.

There is no need to put *Referees available on request* on the CV either. Waste of CV space – employers **know** they can get them from you if they want them.

However, for recent graduates and career starters employers like to see the name and contact details of a lecturer/tutor/teacher on one of the courses. If you have had a part-time job it is worth including the name and contact details of your manager there also.

31

Same CV rules for all countries? Of course not

Bit of a minefield, in fact. It's standard in some countries to include your date of birth on the CV while in others employers will strongly discourage and even ignore CVs with a date of birth on it in case they are accused of age discrimination. Including a photo on your CV when applying for a job in Ireland or the UK will be viewed as inappropriate but not including one when applying for a job in Germany will probably mean you won't be considered for an interview. And yes, it's true that including a photo on your LinkedIn profile is highly recommended and will lead to more views of your profile. And it's also true that it's a good idea to include your LinkedIn url on your CV. It doesn't take advanced sleuthing skills to click on the profile link on your CV and see your profile photo, so what's the big deal? It's all about knowing what employers expect and what they view as acceptable. Why does it have to be so complicated?

To help you navigate the global jobs market we have summarised the main differences for the CV sections we are asked about most frequently.

Applying for a job in...	Pages in CV	Photo	Date of Birth	Place of birth	Nationality	Marital Status	Postal Address
UK	2	No	No	No	No	No	Optional
Ireland	2	No	No	No	No	No	Optional
USA	1	No	No	No	No	No	Optional
Poland	2	Yes	Usually included	Yes	Yes	Optional	Yes
Netherlands	2	Not usually included	Optional	Optional	Not essential – optional	Not essential	Yes
Spain	1 to 2	Recommended	Yes	Usually included	Yes	Usually included	Yes
France	1 to 2	Optional	Yes	Yes	Yes	Optional	Yes
Portugal	1 to 2	Recommended	Yes	Yes	Yes	Optional	Yes
Germany	1 to 2	Yes	Optional	Optional	Not essential but usual	Usually included	Yes
Sweden	1 to 2	Not usually included	Yes	Optional	No	No	Yes
Italy	1 to 2	Not usually included	Yes	Yes	Yes	Yes	Yes
Australia	2	No	No	No	No	No	Optional

32

The Europass CV . . .
Great idea or bland and outdated?

If you haven't heard of the Europass CV don't waste time figuring out what it is and if you need it. This is all you need to know:

A) It's an attempt to provide a standard format across all European countries so that it is easier for employers to figure out how relevant your experience, education and skills are in their country. It is constructed using an online wizard.

B) It looks terrible and includes information that is not relevant or interesting to employers. AVOID. Write your own CV where you are in control of what you put in it. Use the guide on page 45 to figure out what you need to put on your CV if you are applying for a job outside your home country.

33

Does a picture really paint a thousand words? What's the story with infographic CVs?

You've probably seen them popping up on social media sites. Stylish and visually appealing, they use a combination of colour, icons and a few graphs or pie charts thrown in to illustrate your work experience and skills. If they are done well (that's a big IF) they can look great. You are more likely to see them used for roles in creative or tech industries. There are lots of free online templates you can use to prepare an infographic CV. If you are trying this out for the first time prepare to set aside A LOT of time creating your masterpiece.

And even if you are convinced that yours is the best looking infographic CV ever produced we would recommend that you don't ditch your original CV in favour of its cooler infographic cousin. Use it to complement your traditional CV rather than replace it. The infographic can be a great conversation topic when you are in the interview – **but you still need to get in there first**. Employers (even the creative and tech firms) still like the familiarity of the traditional CV format. Another reason for not abandoning the more conventional CV format and for adopting a dual CV approach is that the ATS may struggle to read and interpret all of your fancy graphs. Because it can't figure out what the charts are saying it could conclude that you don't have the required experience to be shortlisted. Computer says NO.

34

Cover letters – do I even need one?

Helpful answer time again: it depends. Writing cover letters can be a painful process and, let's face it, most people will avoid it if they think they can get away with it. We had a client once who admitted that their job search strategy post graduating from university was to only apply for jobs that **didn't** ask them to include a cover letter with their CV. Not a great strategy.

Do you need a cover letter if:

1. The job advert asks you to apply with your CV **and cover letter**
Yes – why are you even asking? Give them what they want.

2. You are responding to a job listing from a jobs board or agency which just says 'Apply with CV'
No – waste of time – they probably won't even read it

3. You are completing an online application form and one of the questions is 'why are you suitable for this role?'
No – the answer to this question is the same as the content of your cover letter. You don't need to say it twice.

4. An employer (not agency) has advertised a job and the advert says – apply with your CV. They don't specifically mention a cover letter.

Yes – 50% of employers will read them and 50% won't. You have no idea which camp this company is in. Play it safe – write one.

5. You are sending out speculative CVs to employers who currently don't have any jobs advertised.

Yes. Just sending a CV is a waste of time. They want to know why you are contacting them. Give them some context in the cover letter.

35

Here's my cover letter. I've used the same one for five years

A one-size-fits-all generic cover letter is worse than none at all. Employers can spot them a mile off and it shouts:

'I couldn't be bothered to take the time to write anything directly tailored to you or your company. I don't even need to know your name. I think I'm great. Please give me a job.'

And then you're wondering why you haven't heard back from them.

'Bloody employers, all the same, no respect for candidates.'

Cover letters need to have some **love** and **attention** directed at the employer. Employers want to know that it was written specifically for them. Borrowing a phrase from Dale Carnegie, 'the sweetest sound to someone is the sound of their own name' . . . or their company's name as whoever is reading your cover letter has probably worked extremely hard to make it successful. In your cover letter use the company name at least three times. Mention a recent company development and how you are interested in it. An employer told us recently that of the twenty-plus speculative CVs they receive each week from people looking for a job, they only interview the ones that had included a cover letter with evidence that the candidate had done some research about the company – one or two lines would do the trick – it just needed to be there. The candidate who congratulated them on winning an industry award the month before was put to the top of the pile. Everyone loves praise – even employers.

Hilt guide to the 5 paragraph, 1 page cover letter.

Paragraph	What to include
1 (4 lines)	**Short Introduction:** Mention the role you're applying for and their company name. Give a one line summary of your relevant experience and education.
2 (8 lines)	Summarise your **Work Experience.** Mention how and why it's relevant to the role you're applying for. Mention their company name.
3 (8 lines)	Summarise your **Education** – if relevant. If it's been a long time since you were in Education or you don't have much to say about this section then omit it and add another Work Experience paragraph.

Paragraph	What to include
4 (4 lines)	**Skills and Competencies**. Examine the job description. Look at what they want – and **tell them that you have them**. E.g. *'In my current role at Green & Co I have demonstrated that I have excellent problem-solving skills and can quickly assess complex situations and make decisions. I know that these skills are extremely important in this role at Red & Co.'*
5 (3 lines)	**Strong Finish**. It's all about what you can do for them, not about what you want for yourself. Employers **don't care** that this job would be a great opportunity for you to increase your knowledge or experience or use the degree you worked so hard to get. Don't finish with that. Don't sound desperately grateful that they have even read your cover letter. Finish on a strong note. Back yourself. Tell them you know that you can make a significant contribution to their company and you would really like the opportunity to discuss this at an interview.

36

Please apply using a video cover letter

What did you just say? As the name indicates, a video cover letter is a recording of you introducing yourself and telling the employer what you can offer the role and why you want to work for them. Not too commonplace at present but watch this space as employers are starting to figure out just how much information they can get about you at the application stage from a one or two minute video.

Don't be tempted to video record yourself just reading your actual cover letter and send them that. Boring. Use the five paragraphs of your cover letter as a structure for what you are going to say but make sure that you deliver it in a way that makes you sound engaged and interested in the company and in what you are saying about yourself. To make a strong impact keep your eyes on the camera – not on your notes. Monotone deliveries will send them off to sleep. Nor do you want to go overboard and rap your way through your script with Eminem as a backing track. Somewhere in between those two will be fine. One thing is pretty much guaranteed – the first take will be awful – as will the second, third, fourth . . . Keep practising and get to know your way around the video editing software on your computer. See 52 for more advice on completing video interviews.

37

Competency based application form

You are all set to send them your CV and cover letter to apply for a job. Except they don't want it. Instead they want you to complete a twenty-page online application form. What's that all about?

Competency based application forms start off looking like a version of your CV. They ask you to fill in a section about your Work Experience, list the jobs and what you did in each job. Then they will ask about your Education. So far so normal. And just when you were wondering why people hate competency based application Forms so much you see Section B. Here they will list up to five competencies that are key to doing the job and ask you to describe (usually in less than 300 words) a time when you demonstrated each one.

Typical questions on a competency based application form would be:

Demonstrate your experience of working on your own initiative as part of a team to manage complex projects and deliver clear results.
Competency being tested: Contributing to teams

Summarise your experience of anticipating and evaluating problems and taking action when faced with potential obstacles.
Competency being tested: Proactive problem solving

Before you decide that completing this form is just FAR too much trouble and you never really wanted that job anyway let's play Bad News/Good News.

Bad News: We're going to be honest here. Trudging through your memory banks to recall scenarios and then writing up the answers to the competency questions on these forms is pretty torturous work. At a conservative estimate it will take you at least forty-five minutes per competency – and most forms will have at least four competencies. Coffee time.

Good News: Once you have completed the form you will have also done the bulk of the work for preparing for your interview. Two for the price of one. So by diligently completing the application form what you are doing is FRONTLOADING the work. You will have to do it anyway for the interview – it's just timing. And if that isn't convincing you to tackle the form and apply for the job, consider this. Competency based interviews are entirely predictable. They will ask you questions to prove that you have the same competencies you wrote about in your application form. It's like being handed your exam paper a few weeks before your exam – well, kind of.

38

How to structure your answers for competency based application forms

- Keep to the allotted word count. Anything over it may be chopped off your answer without you knowing it.
- Divide the answer into three paragraphs and use the STARR method to structure your answers – Situation/Task, Action, Result/Reflection – see 70-71.
- Numbers and statistics give better evidence than words to prove what you did was successful. For example:

As a result of my initiative to introduce the new system for dealing with customer queries the team has reduced the time spent dealing with queries each week by eight hours while maintaining the same customer satisfaction levels of 96%.

Rather than:

My initiative to introduce the new system for dealing with customer queries has led to increased efficiencies within the team.

- You could give two short examples rather than one longer one.
- Don't use the same Situation/Task for two different competency questions.

• Keep your examples to things that happened in the last three years. Recounting a story of you showing initiative seven years ago will have them wondering if you have ever shown it since then!

39

Turning a CV into a resume

Getting a two-page CV into a one-page resume involves more than just reducing the font size and the page margins.

The aim of both is the same – to inform the employer and sell yourself into the job. A resume is designed to give a chronology of each relevant job you have had and a **brief summary** of what you achieved in each whereas a CV will give more detail about your activities and achievements in every job. Think six bullet points to describe a job on a CV and two or three for the same job on a resume.

The section headings will be the same on both. Leading with your best cards is just as relevant when you are writing your resume.

40

Going for the chop.
After all of this your CV is still four
pages. Tips for getting it to two

✓   Your personal details – name and contact details should take no more than three lines

Jason Job

E: jason@XXXXX.com   M: XXX XXX XXX
www.linkedin.com/en/xxxx

✓   Group similar jobs from earlier in your career together – see 21.

✓   Give less page space to jobs you had more than ten years ago – one or two bullet points should suffice for each 'older' job. For some of your first jobs it will be enough to just state the job title, employer and years you held the role – no other description is required.

✓   Don't let a bullet point run over to another precious line for the sake of a word or two – find another way to say the same thing in one line.

✓   When listing technical skills list them in three or four parallel columns rather than one long list. It's okay to go down a font size for that.

✓ Reduce the font to 10.5 (don't go lower) and also reduce the margins but not less than 1.5 for any of them.

✓ Delete the Referees details – employers know they can ask you for them when they want them.

YOUR INTERVIEW

41

What's the purpose of the interview?

Your CV was great. It told them you have what they are looking for. It has made them want to meet you. CV. Job. Done. But now you need to tell them all of that again – in person this time. Your CV got you into the room but that's the end of its power. It's over to you now to convince them that you can deliver on what you have claimed in the CV.

Interviewers have lots of questions. A quick Google search[1] will give you a ridiculously unhelpful list of hundreds of commonly asked interview questions for you to lose sleep over – but they all come down to interviewers wanting to know three things – what you have, how you will apply it to the role and why you want to work for them.

WHAT INTERVIEWERS WANT TO KNOW...

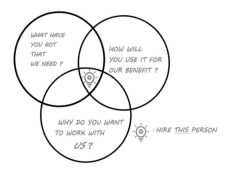

WHAT HAVE YOU GOT THAT WE NEED ?

HOW WILL YOU USE IT FOR OUR BENEFIT ?

WHY DO YOU WANT TO WORK WITH US ?

: HIRE THIS PERSON

---

[1] For your sanity and to ensure an all-round good interview performance we don't recommend this approach. See 64 for a better way.

Every question they will ask you and every assessment they will make you do will be linked to them getting the answers to questions they have relating to these three areas. Stay focused on this bigger picture when you are preparing for the interview.

42

You are not a mindreader. Ask them what to expect

All interviews have the same aim – to figure out if you have what they are looking for. But employers use lots of different interview formats and techniques to reach that decision. From traditional to video interviews and everything in between. When inviting you for an interview some employers will tell you exactly what to expect. E.g. *'You will have a competency based interview with the Head of HR followed by a technical interview with the Engineering Director.'* Other employers keep the interview type details vague or non-existent – *'Please attend for an interview on Tuesday 10th at 2.00 p.m.'* **Subtext:** Use your best powers of intuition and forecasting or some online forum where people share horror stories of their interviews with us to figure out what to expect.

If you are not sure what format the interview will take, **enquire when you get the invitation**. Ask them who will be interviewing you and what their roles in the company are. Know what – and who – you are up against – it will help your preparation. The questions the HR representative will ask you will be different than those asked by the line of business manager. You need to know what to expect.

Let's take a look at the different types of interview formats used by employers.

43

Competency interview

Been around forever and by far the most widely used interview format by both public and private sector employers. Before the interview employers identify several (usually between four and six) key characteristics the successful candidate needs to have and then ask the candidate to prove that they have them. Sounds straightforward?

Pros: Relatively easy to figure out what competencies are on the employer's hit list. There are widely known and well established methods to structure your answers and give them what they are looking for.

Cons: Practically impossible to wing it and get away with it. Requires you to put in the hours in advance of the interview to recall scenarios and practise your answers.

What to do: Use the job description to anticipate the questions they will ask – and then practise your answers out loud. See 64.

44

Technical interview

You will be interviewed by a subject matter expert in the area you are applying for – more than likely the person you would be reporting to. They will ask you questions to prove you know the day-to-day requirements for the job.

For example:

For an accounting interview: *We use the Elite Enterprise Reporting System (ERP) here. What experience do you have of this system?*

For a digital marketing interview: *What do you think would be the three most effective digital marketing tools for a start-up business in the food industry?*

For a social care interview: *What are the main regulations and legislation that govern the area of childcare and child protection?*

You get the idea.

Pros: You are doing this stuff every day in your current role or you have just finished a qualification where you have been learning all about it. You know this. Most candidates find this one of the most straightforward types of interview.

Cons: There's always the risk that they ask you something that you should know but don't. Or it has been so long since you looked at it you used to know it but have forgotten all of it.

What to do: Consolidate what you know and be able to comprehensively explain what you do on a day to day basis in your current role. Review your CV and remind yourself of what you did in your previous jobs. '*What systems did you use when you worked at ReadyCard?*' is a fairly straightforward question. But if you left that job five years ago and haven't thought about it since you will struggle to convince them that you even worked there. Do your homework but be realistic. Don't put yourself under pressure to know absolutely everything. There are ways to tell them 'I don't know the answer to that question' without looking like an idiot. See 90.

45

Whiteboard interview

Used almost exclusively for technology roles or roles requiring analytical skills. The interviewer asks you to work your way through solving a problem or write some code using a whiteboard, blank sheet of paper, computer or, worst of all, just your brain. You've told them in your CV that you are brilliant at writing code – so prove it – now. They want you to talk about the steps you are taking as you are doing it. Chalk-and-talk time.

Pros: Great if you are a good communicator and can explain to them what you are doing as you solve the problem. Allows for good two-way interaction with the interviewer. You can ask the interviewer questions along the way to clarify things.

Cons: If you're not used to speaking in public there is definite potential for brain freeze leading to panic and a large amount of sweating. There's a chance that what was easy to explain yesterday when you were sitting at home practising to the wall becomes almost impossible to say when you are standing in the interview room with a big shiny empty whiteboard staring at you waiting to be written on. A client of ours recently told us of their experience with a whiteboard interview when they were interviewing for a risk analyst role. Sitting casually across the table from them the interviewer said that they were going to ask them to do some mental arithmetic. Started off easy . . . What's 7 x 9? What's 11 x 13? Before shifting into the sweaty palm and getmeoutofhere territory: What's 23 x 14? What's 245 x 21? What's 2,130 x 17? And on went the torture until our client's brain went into brainfreeze mode. Not a good experience.

What to do: Simulate the conditions as closely as possible prior to the interview. Use a whiteboard or stick some paper on the wall and practise explaining a process to a friend while drawing the steps on the board. Don't stand with your back to them hunched over the whiteboard scribbling like a maniac. They want to see and hear your thought process. It should be as close as you can get to a two-way conversation being led by you.

46

Strengths-based interview

These are slowly gaining popularity as a way for employers to get past the pre-prepared answers to competency questions and find out what really makes you tick. So rather than asking you questions to figure out what you are good at they will ask you questions to figure out what you enjoy doing (in a work context) – not always the same thing! Their thinking is if you enjoy doing it you will be energised and will do it well. Let's figure out if what you enjoy doing matches what we need. Typical questions would be:

Are you a starter or a finisher?
What are you good at?
What gives you energy or motivation?
What does a great day at work look like to you?

Pros: They want short snappy answers so there is no need to prepare lots of scenarios to offer as evidence. They are really looking for you to give them a well thought out summary of your key strengths and how they would be of benefit to their company. A high level of self awareness, motivation and enthusiasm for what you are saying is what they are after. If you can't show enthusiasm when talking about yourself and what you're good at then chances are you probably won't demonstrate it when doing tasks associated with the job.

Cons: Relies more on you thinking on your feet than having the security of your well thought through and well rehearsed answers to competency questions. As your answers will be short (max thirty seconds) they will have time to ask more questions than in a traditional competency based interview. Still requires a lot of preparation as you need to figure out what the company needs and see if that matches your strengths.

What to do: Do you homework on the company. Look at the job spec – what strengths have they said they want? Think about how you match what they are looking for. Do a personality assessment or strengths profile test online to get you thinking about and finding descriptions of your key strengths. Ask a colleague or someone who knows you well to tell you what they think your key strengths are. You may be surprised at the results.

Don't be tempted to give them the answer you think they want to hear. For example:

Interviewer: *'Are you more of a big picture or detail person?'*

You think to yourself: *Okay, this is a finance firm. They will probably be more interested in the detail-oriented person. I'm known to be pretty terrible at all that but I better say I'm great at it.*

Don't do it. You might fool them into giving you the job and you will hate it.

47

Market sizing interview

Even the seemingly wacky questions asked in a market sizing interview – e.g. how many straws are used each day in the USA or what is the market size of the surf board market in Australia have a purpose that can be traced back to the requirements of the job. A market sizing interview tests your ability to work with ambiguity and make sensible assumptions under pressure.

What to do: Make sure you understand exactly what they are asking you to do. Ask clarification questions until you are sure about what you are calculating.

Avoid panicking and blurting out the first thing that comes to mind when asked something you clearly couldn't know the correct answer to.

There will be a whiteboard or paper available for you to use so use it. Write out your key assumptions and the key estimated figures you are going to work off.

For example, if you were trying to estimate the size of the surf board market in Australia you would be making assumptions about:

- Population of Australia
- % of population who buy a surf board each year
- Average retail price of a surf board

• Purchases of surfboards by organisations/visitors to the country

None of your assumptions will be correct, but that's okay. As long as they pass the common sense test then you are on the right track. Take a step back and apply a sanity check to your figures as you go along. Round the numbers as you go through the calculations. They are looking for ballpark sensible estimates rather than pinpoint accuracy (which is impossible, so don't even try it).

48

Internal promotion interview

'I'm being interviewed by people who already know just how amazing I am – do I even need to show up?'

Pros: No scary unknown interviewers and you will have a really good idea of what is involved in the job since you have been working for the company for a while now.

Cons: Our clients tell us that it is much more difficult to interview with people you know well. Less opportunity to big yourself and your achievements up – they know the truth about how that project you worked on for two years ended up. There is nowhere to hide.

What to do: Even if you know FOR A FACT that your boss thinks you're amazing, don't assume you are a shoo-in for the job. Tell yourself that the interviewer(s) know NOTHING about you and may as well have just landed here from another planet. Explain each detail of the project to them even though they may have worked on that project with you. They need to hear evidence in the interview. They are taking notes on what you are saying. If you didn't say it . . . it didn't happen.

49

The clueless interviewer interview

Your interviewer has never interviewed anyone before and has no idea how to do it.

Not all companies have the support and expertise of an HR department to advise how to plan and structure an interview. For start-ups and smaller firms chances are you will be interviewed by one of the founders or owners. What if they don't have much experience of interviewing people? A sure-fire giveaway is when they start stabbing at stuff on your CV saying, '*Tell me about this*' or '*What did you do in this job*' or '*I see you worked in ABC Co – what was that like?*' Basically they are using your CV as their interview question prompt script.

Pros: None really. Sometimes the interviewer can be more nervous than the candidate. Not ideal. The interview lasted forty-five minutes and thirty-five of those were taken up by the interviewer telling you all about how they started the company. They have learned very little about you.

Cons: Given their limited line of questioning, you may not get the opportunity to tell them everything you had planned. You have lots of examples ready to go about times when you showed all of the competencies they are looking for but so far all they've done is work their way down your CV checking facts and dates as they went. This will also make it difficult for them to accurately compare one candidate to another. Help them out.

What to do: During the interview, once you come to the conclusion that it is going nowhere fast, politely ask if it would be useful if you gave them a summary of what your key strengths are and why they would be of benefit to the role. See 74 for how to structure your answer to Tell Me About Yourself. They will bite your hand off. And then they will probably offer you the job out of sheer gratitude that you took control of the situation and took them out of their interviewing misery.

50

Phone interview

Most phone interviews will be scheduled in advance and you'll get plenty of notice – '*We will call you at 2 p.m. on Tuesday 10th.*' Occasionally the recruiter may call you without warning to follow up on your application. '*Hi there, I received your CV and wanted to ask you a few questions about your experience. Is now a good time?*' **STOP**. If you are not in a place where you can concentrate on giving them good answers then suggest you call them back later that day. Hiding in the office stairwell while trying to sell yourself by explaining what your key career achievements are, hoping no one can hear you, is a poor job interview strategy. Don't sabotage your chances of getting to the next interview.

Prepare for a phone interview in the same way as you would prepare for a face-to-face interview. When doing a phone interview dress to impress – **yourself**. Just because the interviewer can't see you doesn't mean you shouldn't dress as if they can. You may think it is slightly ridiculous to sit at your kitchen table or in your bedroom all dressed up in your best interview gear while you talk to them on the phone. But do it. It will get your brain into the zone for the interview, sharpen your responses and is likely to have a positive effect on your performance.

Prior to the interview, do a few tests calls to friends from the phone and location where you plan to do the interview.

If your friends can't hear you properly then switch location, device or both. Nothing annoys an interviewer more than a choppy phone line. They will assume the bad connection is on your side and may not give you a second chance.

51

Skype interview

Newsflash: they can see you – and everything/everyone around you. Watch your background. Things that you thought were off-camera will sneak into the frame. Test your camera and do a trial run to see what they can see when they are Skyping you. We have sat through many Skype interviews where the candidate had done such a lousy job of lighting themselves for the camera that it was almost impossible to recognise any facial features whatsoever. Just a voice coming from a dark patch on the screen. No one is hiring that. Fix your lighting . . . and check your sound while you are at it.

If you don't use Skype regularly, allow plenty of time to get logged in. Skype has a fairly regular habit of upgrading the service which requires you to install a new version and remember the original password you set and haven't used for two years. This is the last thing you want to be doing when you are ten minutes away from the interview start time. Sort your tech out plenty of time in advance.

While you will be tempted to look at the interviewer's picture on your screen, remember that you only make eye contact with them when you look at the camera. Put a sticky note beside (not over!) your camera with ***Look Here!*** written on it to remind you to maintain eye contact.

Once you have all this sorted prepare for this as you would a face-to-face interview.

52

Video interview – I may as well be talking to the wall

Many people will use the terms 'video interview' and 'Skype interview' interchangeably and assume they are the same. They are not.

A **Skype interview** is a face-to-face interview conducted in real time with an interviewer or interview panel via a live video link. A **video interview** is a one-way interview where you use your laptop, desktop, phone or tablet to record your answers to a set of between four and eight interview questions that appear on your screen one after another. They will be a mix of fairly predictable competency, technical and motivational questions.

You are emailed a link and you are given up to seventy-two hours to click on it and record your answers to their questions. There is no one watching your answers in real time. You are talking to yourself. It can be a lonely and uncomfortable place. Once you have completed and sent the interview to the employer, they will watch your pre-recorded video and assess your answers – over popcorn, with colleagues if they feel like it. Most employers will not give you a chance to re-record an answer if you mess it up. It's a one-time recording – no second takes.

Employers love video interviews as they reduce the time to hire and cost of hiring by a whopping 75%. They tell us the candidates **also** love video interviews because of the flexibility of being able to complete the video interview at any time during the seventy-two-hour window. *'If you want to complete your video interview at 4 a.m. while on holiday 4,000 miles away from our office – well that's alright with us.'* But candidates tell us that the video interview experience is both convenient **and terrifying** in equal measure.

When you are doing a video interview the advice on getting your technology, lighting and background right is the same as it is for Skype interviews. They need to be able to see and hear you. Depending on the employer, some video interviews are analysed by Artificial Intelligence (AI). An algorithm developed in consultation with the employer will analyse your facial expressions, eye movements, tone of your voice, body language and keyword choice and come to a swift conclusion as to whether you are worth meeting in person. Knowing that you are talking to a robot who will be making a 'decision' on whether you are a good fit for the company can add an extra layer of weirdness to the video interview process.

53

Quick chat

Q: When is a quick chat not a quick chat?

A: When it's with a potential employer. This is an interview. As a result of this seemingly casual chat they will decide whether or not to proceed with your application. Be prepared.

54

Coffee shop interview

Someone from a company you are interested in working for calls you and says, '*Hey, I hear that you may be interested in working here. Let's meet for coffee and discuss how this might work.*' Beware. This is code for: '*Let's meet so I can ask you questions in a setting that is nice and relaxing and will fool you into thinking that this is not a real interview.*' It **is** a real interview. You don't need to turn up in your interview suit ready to rhyme off your answers to commonly asked competency questions but you do need to be able to summarise what you think you can bring to the role. Research their company and have an idea of what you could offer them.

And if they invited you for coffee – you don't need to offer to pay. Leave first and say thanks. That'll do.

55

Presentation

The email is titled **Invitation to Interview.** It looks promising. You click it open and read this:

Congratulations. You have been selected for a final round interview for ABC Co. As part of the assessment process and prior to the commencement of the interview you are requested to give a ten minute presentation on the topic of 'Opportunities for expansion into international markets'. Please email your presentation slides to us two days before the interview date.

Well that's just GREAT. You hate speaking in public and the thought of presenting to a room of interviewers is sending you into a panic. OK, think about it this way. The first ten minutes of the process to assess how good you are will now be entirely dictated by you. There are no uncertainties. You will deliver a presentation written by you and you will know the content extremely well. Ten whole minutes of familiar, predictable, solid ground at the beginning of the interview process where you show them what you know about the role – who wouldn't want that? Are we convincing you yet that it's a good idea?

Clearly employers don't know that people generally fear speaking in public even more than they fear death. Or maybe they do. Here are some tips for delivering a presentation as part of the interview process:

• Just as you were told before sitting every exam you've ever done – READ THE QUESTION. What exactly are they asking you to present on? Clarify with them if you are not sure.

• Go easy on the slide content – less is more. Use diagrams and visuals. Interviewers can't read your slides and listen to you at the same time.

• Each slide will take an average of two minutes to talk though. For a ten minute presentation that means five or six slides – not seventeen, as we saw recently.

• Talk to them – not the screen and not the laptop.

• Notes are okay – having a few keywords written on index cards make you look like you know what you are doing.

• Remember the three Ts of presentations:

    o **T**ell them what you are going to tell them, then

    o **T**ell them, then

    o **T**ell them what you have told them

    o *Over and out*

56

Who will be interviewing me? One person or a panel?

Find out in advance who is interviewing you. If they can't/won't give you the names of the interviewers (they don't have to) then at least find out if it will be one person or more than one, i.e. a panel interview. You don't want to walk into the interview room expecting one interviewer and find four sitting in front of you. Bad start.

In a panel interview, who should you look at when answering the questions? We get asked this a lot. Target your answer and eye contact at whoever has asked you the question. Throughout your answer you can glance occasionally at the other interviewers but chances are at least one of them will be writing what you are saying and won't look up. That's okay. They ARE listening to you.

57

Group interview

Imagine that all of the other interview candidates you are competing against were allowed to sit in on your interview and listen to your answers. Maybe even take some of what you have said and use it to build on their own answers. Welcome to the group interview.

Frequently used by employers for roles that involve dealing with the public – e.g. retail, hospitality, customer contact centres – employers use them as a relatively cost-effective way to assess up to ten candidates at one time. Sound like an ordeal? It is, and you should know that this group interview ordeal can take one of two forms.

Group interview – individual questions

You will be invited to sit in a room with all of the other candidates and each of you will be asked questions in turn. Each of you may be asked the same question to start off with and then different questions per candidate as the interview goes on. For example, a typical opening question for a group interview would be: '*Can you describe yourself in three words?*' (And by the way, you get no points for hardworking, honest and punctual – that is baseline and the minimum they expect – be **more ambitious** about yourself, for crying out loud.)

Another question often used to open up a group interview is: '*Why do you want to work here?*' Being the first to speak has an advantage in that what you have planned to say can't be 'taken' by anyone else prior to you speaking. However, it's always useful for you to hear a few answers before they get to you so the ideal position is third or fourth to speak.

Most of the time you don't get a choice about when you answer – whether you're first or last to speak, when it's your turn you need to turn it on. Anticipate the questions in advance of the interview and practise your answers. See 64. Stick to your plan and don't get distracted, overwhelmed or intimidated by what everyone else is saying. You are looking to impress the interviewer or assessors in the room, not the other candidates.

Group interview: group discussion or group task
Employers will ask you and the other candidates to work in a group to discuss a topic given to you on the spot. You will get a short written summary of what is required and you will be given up to ten minutes to read the content before the timed discussion starts. They'll choose a generic topic so no candidate should have an unfair advantage over another.

You are usually asked to agree on a set of conclusions or recommendations by the end of the allotted time. Twenty to thirty minutes is the standard amount of time given for the discussion and it will go by in a flash.

In a group discussion they are rating you across competencies such as: Teamwork, Assertiveness, Leadership, Verbal Communication, Influence and Empathy. The job you are interviewing for requires all of these, so it stands to reason that this is what they will be looking for.

We have worked with hundreds of candidates who have participated in group discussions during the assessment process and they all tell us the same thing: the longer you leave it before you contribute to the discussion the more difficult it is to insert yourself into it. Get out of the starting block early with an '*Okay, we have twenty minutes to decide how to distribute this large donation amongst three of ten potential worthy causes. Why don't I keep the time and give us a recap every five minutes or so as to what we have achieved?*' Genius. Everyone in the room is now looking at you and wishing they'd said that. You sound in control but helpful, collaborative, and focused on the task all at the same time. You're off to a great start and you'll have the assessors nodding approvingly in your direction. Encourage others to join the discussion – including people by actively seeking their opinion is exactly what the assessors are looking for. If they haven't given you name badges, suggest that everyone writes their name on a piece of paper and use their name when you are talking to people. 'That's a good idea, Mike,' sounds like you are much more engaged in the conversation than just saying, 'Good idea.'

The loudest or most consistent voice in the room is not always (or hardly ever) the one that makes the biggest *positive* impact on the assessors. But let's face it, if you sit there for twenty minutes watching the conversation go by and say nothing you are making zero impression. You will be an easy NO.

58

Assessment centre

An assessment centre is an intense day-long series of activities and interviews to determine if you or the seven other candidates invited with you are a good fit for the role. You will have completed at least one screening interview with the company prior to being invited to the assessment centre. Assessment centres are expensive for companies to run. You will not be invited unless they think you have a strong chance of doing well and being offered a job. They won't waste their time and money on long shots. We have observed some assessment centres where six of the eight candidates were given job offers and others where none of the eight candidates were selected. You're competing against yourself.

You will be put through your paces by completing a number of tasks and interviews back-to-back. The tasks will be a mix of individual and group activities. While the exact tasks will vary, depending on the company and role, the example on the following page is a fairly typical agenda for an assessment centre day. One thing we know for certain is that you will be exhausted when the day is finished. Get a good sleep the night before. Make sure your positivity and can-do attitude is noticed. Look like you are enjoying every minute of the day – even if you're not!

09.00–10.00	Competency based interview with HR
10.00–10.45	Skills interview with hiring manager
10.45–11.30	Coffee break – opportunity to network[1] with other candidates and employees
11.30–12.30	Group discussion
12.30–13.30	Lunch with senior managers
13.30–14.00	Preparation for presentation
14.00–14.45	Presentation and Q&A with hiring manager
14.45–15.45	Complete online aptitude tests

---

[1] Everyone in the company who had an interaction with you on the day will be asked for their opinion of you – not just the official interviewers. Be as respectful and friendly to the receptionist and the person who serves you your lunch as you are to the senior partners. Walls have ears.

59

How much time should I spend preparing for an interview?

We ask this question to participants at our interview workshops and still get surprised by the range of answers. We've heard everything from 'at least an hour' to 'about three or four weeks'. We recommended that you spend approximately two business days – fourteen hours – preparing for the interview. You can do a few hours and come back to it – you don't need to lock yourself away and run the fourteen hours straight through! What are you doing in all that time? Quite a lot – read on.

60

When should I start to prepare?

Should you wait until they call or email you to tell you you have an interview? Or kick on with the preparation in the hope that they will? Back yourself here folks.

Let's look at the evidence:
- You KNOW your CV is good.
- You have applied for several jobs in an industry that is actively recruiting.

Based on this evidence, there is a high probability you will be called for an interview. Get ready. While employers in the public sector usually give you seven days' notice of an upcoming interview, there is no minimum notice period legally required from employers. Anything from a three-week run-in to hearing 'is now a good time?' when you answer their phone call is fair game. Why wait until you get confirmation of a time and date? Going into a blind panic as soon as you get the interview invitation email or call is not a great way to start your preparation.

While employers might like to think their interviewing style and technique is individual, unique and very specific to their company we can tell you that approx 70-80% of the questions asked in interviews are the same – regardless of what industry you are interviewing for. Prepare well for one and you have done a lot of the groundwork for all of them. Good deal.

61

I got a call today inviting me to an interview in two days. I'd love this job but I'm not ready for the interview.

Can I tell them I am not available on that day? Buy myself some time to prepare? Of course. Always worth a try. It might work and as long as you say that it is due to a scheduling conflict (rather than a version of '*Whaaat the hell? Two days from now? Are you kidding me? Can I have a few more days to get myself up to speed?*') they will see what they can do. But be prepared for them to say that the interview panel is only meeting on that day or they need someone ASAP so it's that day or not at all.

62

Okay, I get it. I need to prepare for my interview. How do I do that?

First let's get the absolute worst way to prepare for an interview out of the way. Unfortunately this is what most people do when they are starting to prepare. Let's face it, right now the only thing you're thinking about is what questions you will be asked. You turn to Google and ask it to search for **Most Frequently Asked Interview Questions**. Google never shirks from a challenge and will respond in a flash with a list of at least a hundred questions. For starters. You may narrow the search down to try to make the questions more relevant to your job – **Most Frequently Asked Interview Questions *for Engineering***. You'll still get far too many and most of them won't be in the slightest bit relevant to the job you are interviewing for. You need a better way. What about websites like Glassdoor where candidates post reviews of their interviews and may even list a few questions they were asked? Okay – let's pause and take a moment.

Did you ever have a dream about finding an exam paper left somewhere by accident a few days before your exam? Everything you need to know right there in front of you and not a person in sight. We defy anyone not to have a sneaky look and walk away – cool as you like. The probability of you getting the lowdown on all of the questions you will be asked in an interview by looking up interview report websites is about as high as finding the exam paper left casually on the photocopier. And that probability is practically zero. So stop waiting for a miracle or wasting time by Googling 'typical' questions for that company or industry and do your own targeted and relevant research.

63

Now let's talk about the right way to prepare

It's pretty simple. Employers want **evidence** of how well you can do what's on the job description. Your CV claims that you can do it – that's what got you the interview. But they are not going to believe that you are excellent at making decisions and solving problems or dealing with difficult clients unless you **can tell them about a time you did that in the past**. To do a great interview you need to:

- Figure out what they want.
- FIND THE EVIDENCE of you having that in your career and life to date.
- Tell them about it in a structured and focused way.

That's it. This is not rocket science. It's a process that, if done properly, will practically guarantee that you can answer any question they put to you in an interview. And all you need is time, a highlighter tool and your memory. So let's get started.

64

Looking for question clues? Start with a forensic investigation of the job description

Get the job description and a highlighter. Go through the **Responsibilities, Experience Required** and **Competencies Required** sections of the job description line by line. What does the Job Description tell you the successful candidate should have? This is what they will be testing at your interview – not some random questions pulled from a Google search.

Here is a fairly typical job description. Let's examine and **highlight it** for clues on how to prepare for this interview . . .

Job Description for Project Manager – Financial Services

A: Main Responsibilities:

- Create and manage all project **documentation** including MS project plans, **business cases**, documentation and project **charters**
- Agree project deliverables with key **stakeholders** and ensure **governance**
- Build **relationships** with internal stakeholders and third party suppliers
- Work closely with IT to deliver continuous **business performance** while **controlling costs** and deliverables

• Facilitate information sessions to ensure the **business requirements** are identified and documented
• Ensure progress is documented and communicated to the business, including to **board level** executives

B: Qualifications and Experience Required:

• Demonstrable project management experience, ideally gained within the financial services field
• **Prince 2** or **Agile** Certified (current)
• A proven record of accomplishment in delivering a diverse range of change technology projects using Agile and Prince 2 project methodologies

C: Competencies Required:

• Ability to **multi-task** and handle multiple **tasks and projects simultaneously**
• **Initiative** to achieve all project deliverables and the ability to **work autonomously with minimum supervision**
• Ability to **manage and motivate a small team**
• Highly **organised** with an ability to **adapt** to changing needs and excellent attention to detail
• First-class **decision making** and **influencing** skills
• Excellent communication skills with the ability to clearly **communicate issues, ideas and concepts** both verbally and in written form

Highlight all of the **keywords**. If you don't have a job description or can't find it since you applied for this job months ago and you are only getting called for interview now – contact them and get one. And if that doesn't work see if you can find someone on LinkedIn who is doing a similar job and see how they describe what they do. You need that information to predict the interview questions. (You may want to engage the private mode in LinkedIn's profile viewing if you want to keep the reasons for your detective work to yourself.)

Sections A and B

First off they will look for evidence of **A** and **B on your CV**. If it's not there it's unlikely you will even get called for an interview. The first set of questions in the interview will involve you describing your experience of doing what's listed in A and B. This could be tested via a separate technical or whiteboard interview or could be the opening questions of a competency or strengths-based interview. You will be asked to summarise or explain what you do in your current and previous jobs and explain how it's relevant to the job you are interviewing for now. Or they could get more specific and may pick a requirement of the job and ask what your experience of it is. For example:

> *'Can you tell us about a change technology project you have managed and delivered using Agile and Prince 2 methodologies?'*

Given that this requirement is stated **in the job description** you should not be surprised that they are asking it. Whether they are zoning in on a specific requirement or asking you to summarise what you have done so far in your career, all of the questions they will ask on Sections A and B are looking for validation and clarification of your work experience. You can do that.

Section C

Once they are satisfied that you have the right experience and technical knowledge, they will look to determine how well you will do the job and why you want it. To do this they will ask you a series of questions about the competencies we have highlighted in C. Before you can think about how to give great **answers** you need to figure out what the specific competency **questions** will be!

65

You are the interviewer

Put yourself in their shoes. If you were trying to get evidence of how effectively someone could manage and motivate a small team, how would you get it?

Suggestion 1. Follow them around for a week with a clipboard and every time you see them doing it give them a tick on your clipboard. Add up the ticks at the end of the week. Nice idea but clearly totally impractical and you'd probably be arrested for stalking.

Suggestion 2. Ask them to tell you about a time when they did it and then make a judgement on how convincing and effective their evidence is.

The good news is that there are a limited number of different ways they can ask you about a time you managed a team or solved a problem. Think up your own questions to test each of the competencies you have highlighted. Remember that interviews are very predictable. Chances are you will have thought up the same, or at least very similar, questions as your interviewer. Have two possible questions per competency. Use the questions listed in point 66 to get you started. Congratulations. You've just been handed your exam paper a week before your exam.

66

The question is . . .
what are the questions?

Let's assume we are interviewing you for the Financial Services Project Manager job outlined in 64. The interviewer is looking for evidence of your relevant experience, how you would use it in the job and your motivation for wanting the job. Remember:

WHAT INTERVIEWERS WANT TO KNOW...

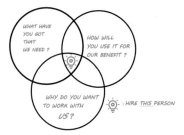

To figure out what you are like as a team leader it would be a waste of time for them to ask you, '*Are you an effective team leader?*' Unless you are a complete idiot you will respond, '*Yes, of course, I'm excellent.*' The problem is they don't believe you – yet. Show them the evidence. Give them an example.

Here are some questions we (and every other interviewer) would ask to test the competencies on this job description. And sure – a version of some of these questions may appear on your Google search of the hundred most commonly asked interview questions. But the difference with this list is that they are specific to the job you're interviewing for. The likelihood of you being asked them at your interview is extremely high. Spend your time on methodical targeted preparation, not scattergun chaos.

	Competency on job description	Possible questions to test this
1	Multitask and handle several projects simultaneously	1. How do you manage multiple deadlines? Tell me about a time when you had to prioritise conflicting demands on your time. 2. Have you ever missed a deadline? What tools and methods do you use to ensure that this doesn't happen (again)?
2	Initiative and working independently	1. Can you describe a time when you took the initiative to improve a process during a project? 2. What is the achievement of which you are most proud?
3	Manage and motivate a team	1. Tell me about a time when you led a team to deliver a successful project. What was important to its success? 2. Describe a time when you needed to motivate a team member that was not performing well in their role.
4	Adaptability	1. Tell us about a time when you needed to adjust quickly to changes that were outside your control. 2. Describe a time when you were persuaded by a colleague to change your approach or method for completing a task.

	Competency on job description	Possible questions to test this
5	Decision making	1. Can you describe a decision you made that you knew was going to be met with resistance? 2. If you have to make a decision between Option A or Option B what factors do you consider? Can you give an example of when you did that?
6	Influence	1. What is the most challenging group of stakeholders/situation you had to gain agreement from for an idea you had? How did you do it? 2. Tell me about a time when you failed to convince someone that your idea was the right one – even though you KNEW it was. What did your learn from this?
7	Communication	1. Describe how you would explain a technical concept to a non-technical audience. Do you have an example of when you have done that in the past? 2. Tell us about a challenging communication you had with a stakeholder or colleague.

67

Now it's your turn

Use this template to structure your own interview question worksheet for a role you have applied for.

Visit www.wearehilt.com for more worksheets and interview question ideas sorted per competency.

	Competency on job description	Possible questions to test this
1		
2		
3		

	Competency on job description	Possible questions to test this
4		
5		
6		
7		

68

How many is enough?

OK – I've identified seven competencies and thought of two questions per competency. Are you now telling me that I need to prepare answers to at least fourteen different questions, each describing a different scenario? How am I going to find examples for all of those?

It's not as bad as you think. Interviews last between thirty and forty minutes on average. They are not going to ask you **several different** questions on each competency. Chances are, they will ask one question per competency and use the content of your answer as a starting point to ask follow-on questions linked to what you have told them. The challenge is that you don't know exactly how they will phrase that one question. This is why we recommend you think of at least two differently worded questions to test each competency. It's likely that you can use the same scenario/example to answer both, but you'll need to have all of this thought through before you start the interview. And you were wondering how it could take two days to prepare for an interview?

As soon as the interview is over and you're kicking yourself because you couldn't think of an answer to one of their questions it will suddenly become blindingly obvious to you that the example you had prepared for:

A: *'Tell me about a time you had a difficult decision to make.'*

Would have worked just as well for the one they actually asked you:

B: '*If you have to make a decision between Option A or Option B what factors do you consider? Can you give an example of when you did that?'*

In the interview, your ability to join the dots and figure out that the example you had prepared for A could have easily been used to answer B will be reduced – that's your nerves at work. Do your interview Q&A mix and match before you go in.

69

I know what I *want* to say – how do I make it sound like an interview answer?

Introducing **STARR** (**S**ituation, **T**ask, **A**ction, **R**esult, **R**eflection) – a method for structuring answers to interview questions and your new best friend. We have also seen it described as **CAR** (**C**ontext, **A**ction, **R**esult) or **PAR** (**P**roblem, **A**ction, **R**esult), but they all amount to the same thing. It's a way to divide your answer into three separate sections which will enable you to give the interviewer the maximum amount of **evidence** of your ability to do whatever they are asking you about.

Used properly it will reduce to almost zero the likelihood of you getting sidetracked, forgetting the question or going off on some crazy irrelevant tangent while answering. It's completely essential to your preparation. You will give better answers and interviewers love it when you use it. You can almost see them sigh with relief when they realise that a candidate is going to structure their answers using STARR. If you haven't heard of it until now you're probably wondering how the hell you ever managed to get through an interview without it.

70

Okay, I'm sold on STARR. Tell me more

It should take you no more than two minutes to give your answer using STARR. You are telling them a story with a very definite beginning, middle and end.

How should you **allocate the time when using STARR to answer an interview question**?

TIMING THE STARR

What should I include in each STARR section?

Situation/Task: Give the background and context to the story you are about to tell them. Set the scene for recalling a **real life**

example of when you showed this competency. Explain what you had to achieve or what the issue or problem was. We are often asked by candidates, '*What – you mean – one ACTUAL, SPECIFIC time?*' Yes – that's exactly what we mean. We don't need to know what the weather was doing that day or what you were wearing, but you do need to position the story in the past tense at a point in time and start from there.

Action I Took: This is where you give them the evidence that you have what they want. Tell them what you did to achieve the objective or solve the problem you had outlined above. Take ownership of the Action you took. If you don't start at least three of your sentences in this section with the word '*I*' they may conclude that you are telling the story as an observer rather than an active participant. Stay away from '*We*'. Even when describing a time when you contributed to a team they will want to know what *your* contribution was – not what the team did as a whole.

Result/Reflection: Don't leave them hanging in mid-air wondering what happened at the end of your story. Take control of the finish and describe what the outcome was. They don't all need to be '*and we all lived happily ever after*' endings. Sometimes their question might be about a time when things didn't go according to plan. Comment on what you learned from the experience and what you would do differently if you were going to do it again.

71

Create your own STARR stories

We have prepared a sample answer using STARR to give you an idea of what to include when structuring yours. There is a template on the next page for you to use to structure your own STARR stories. You can also download STARR worksheets from www.wearehilt.com

---

Using the STARR structure

Competency being tested: Initiative

Interview Question: Can you describe a time when you took the initiative to complete a task or improve a process?

Sample Answer using STARR

SITUATION/TASK

I was an Accounts Assistant with BuyMore – a small but rapidly growing office equipment company. I noticed that we were starting to experience a slight fall-off in repeat business from existing clients. The company was expanding with more product lines and services and it was now challenging to keep track of what clients had bought and send reminders to re-order. Our CRM was limited to Excel spreadsheets and no longer fit for purpose. We were missing opportunities but as a small company we did not have the budget to engage consultants to find a solution to the issue.

ACTION I TOOK

- I suggested to my manager that I would investigate how we can be more efficient in how we track customer purchases. I had some experience of this from my previous role at GoodSales.

- I asked the sales staff to email their clients with a follow-up email after each purchase to track customer satisfaction on each transaction.

- I devised a quick and easy 1-5 scale for a number of items such as – Price, Quality of Items, Speed of Delivery, Likelihood to Order from us again. This gave us a very good idea of client vulnerabilities.

- I approached the Head of the School of Computing of a local college and asked if a group of their students would be interested in devising a customer tracking application for the company as part of their college assignment work. The college agreed to this and were delighted that the students were working on a live business project.

- I worked with the college to explain the business need and then gave the students access to information and the sales staff for three hours each week over six weeks.

RESULT/REFLECTION

The application is now live and is working extremely well.

Implementing all of these initiatives led to a 26% increase in sales revenues since they were put in place over three months ago. Customer satisfaction is at 96% up from 73%.

I think this is a good example of where I showed that I can take initiative to solve a problem. I know that this will be extremely important in this role.

Use this worksheet to create your own answer to a competency question. You can download STARR worksheets from www.wearehilt.com

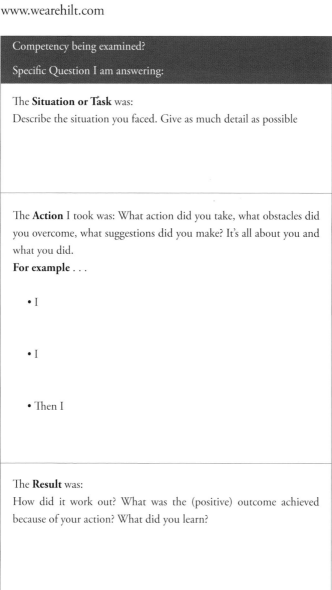

Competency being examined?

Specific Question I am answering:

The **Situation or Task** was:
Describe the situation you faced. Give as much detail as possible

The **Action** I took was: What action did you take, what obstacles did you overcome, what suggestions did you make? It's all about you and what you did.
For example . . .

  • I

  • I

  • Then I

The **Result** was:
How did it work out? What was the (positive) outcome achieved because of your action? What did you learn?

72

Too much information – use Trigger Words

Now that you have STARR on your side you're thinking of great examples and writing them up using the worksheet in 71. You have eight different scenarios all described in detail using the STARR structure. But now you have a new problem. That's a LOT of notes – one full page per scenario and now you're worried that you might forget what scenario/story goes with what competency.

Interviewer: '*Can you describe a time when you dealt with a challenging customer?*'
You: '*Sure, the situation was I was working on a project to roll out a new HR data system for the . . . Oh, sorry, hang on, that's the wrong example. I'll start that again.*'

To help you stay focused, devise a **one page** Trigger Word sheet to clarify what example/scenario matches each competency. When we are working with clients it is often the case that at least one of the stories they tell us could, in theory, be used to prove they have *multiple* competencies. For example, the **Customer App** story used above for proving they can show initiative could also be used as an example of decision making or teamworking skills.

In your Trigger Word sheet put the Trigger Word for that story opposite **all of the relevant competencies**. You can only use this story once in the interview but you now have a choice of *where* to use it. The Trigger Words and their corresponding competencies are what you should be calmly reviewing before you go into the interview, not wading through mountains of notes. If the interviewer asks you about working to deadlines you can run through your register of Trigger Words in your head (they are not going to be impressed if you consult your notes in the interview) and decide what's the best story to tell them. To buy yourself some thinking time, repeat their question back to them when they ask it. *'An example of where I had to work to very tight deadlines? I think a good example of that was when I . . .'* Then deliver your 'Month End and Audit' story using the STARR structure you have prepared.

Sample Trigger Word Sheet

	Competency	Trigger Word
1	Customer Service	Documents signed by deadline
2	Teamwork	Project Orion OR Healthy work committee OR Customer App
3	Initiative	Customer App
4	Working to deadlines	Month end audit
5	Decision making	New staff rotas OR Customer App
6	Leadership	New IT system OR Project Orion

73

You need to talk

Worksheets and Trigger Word sheets are great – but you can't give them to your interviewer and ask them to read them.

You've transferred the ideas for your interview answers from your memory to your worksheets. So far so good. The next stage of your interview preparation is to move your prepared answers from the page and start saying them out loud. Prepare a stack of index cards, each card containing one question from your prepared list of potential interview questions. In our example in 66 that would be fourteen index cards. Ask a (good) friend to pick a few cards at random and pretend to be your interviewer. Ask them to time each of the answers you give them. For competency questions you should be finishing each one within two minutes – less than one minute is definitely too short. Do not attempt to learn your answers off by heart, word for word. You'll be putting yourself under far too much pressure in the interview which will increase your stress levels – and you'll sound like a robot. Just know your stories and be able to tell them in your own words.

If there is no one around to help you practise or if you can't bear to let anyone hear your first attempts, then talk to the wall, to the car windscreen or record yourself on your phone. Whatever way you do it you will need to get used to hearing yourself saying the answers out loud. They will all sound wonderful in your head but their first delivery will be far from perfect. Don't let the interview with the employer be the first time you are road testing your answers out loud.

74

The most asked interview question – EVER

At our interview training workshops we ask participants to guess what question is the most frequently asked interview question in the world. They always get it right. 'Tell me about yourself' or 'Talk me through your CV' wins every time. No surprises there. But what's surprising is how few candidates will prepare a good answer to this question. Many candidates hate being asked it and are unsure of what to include in the answer so avoid preparing for it. Seriously? You KNOW it will be asked. It will be the FIRST question. If you answer it well you can place a virtual halo over your head for the remainder of the interview. Interviewers like candidates who prepare well because it makes their job easier. You have just shown them that you can do that. Consciously or unconsciously they have started to tip the scales in your favour. A good start is half the work and it's looking good for you.

75

Tell me about yourself (TMAY) – what do they want to know?

This seemingly harmless little get-to-know-a-bit-about-you question should be interpreted as follows: '*Tell me how you* ***meet the list of requirements*** *we have on the job description. What do you have that we need? I know you stated on your CV that you had them but I want to hear it coming from you . . . And, by the way, make it sound like you are really interested in working here.*'

But they can't be bothered spelling all that out for you so they hit you with the wildly vague and unhelpful '*Tell me about yourself* ' and expect you to figure all that out for yourself. They do not want you to tell them about your personal life, where you live or what you like to do in your spare time. If it's not relevant to your ability to do the job then they don't care and don't want to hear about it. So what should you tell them? They want a summary of your Work Experience, your Skills relevant to the role, and your Education. Then they would like you to finish it off with a punchy and memorable closing line which leaves them in no doubt that you can do the job. Easy, right?

76

Show me the TMAY template

Use this template overleaf to create the script for your own answer to Tell Me About Yourself. You should be able to finish the answer within two minutes. They will use what you say in this answer as a prompt for asking you questions as the interviewing progresses. Think of what you are telling them in your first answer as a series of headlines in a newspaper, not the entire article. You do not need to squeeze everything you want to tell them in the entire interview into the first answer. Don't put yourself under pressure to do that. You're skimming the surface – the deep dive comes throughout the interview. And because we know you're sitting there thinking, '*Where do I start?*' we have also included a sample answer to get the ball rolling.

Tell Me About Yourself – sample answer

Work Experience Start with your current role and work back. Mention what you have achieved in your current and previous roles and mention how this is relevant to the job your are interviewing for now.	I am a chartered accountant with over twelve years' experience working for a global accountancy practice – ABC Co. I have specialised in tax and fiscal matters and I'm the key contact point for tax for over twenty-five large clients. I have built this client group up from twelve to twenty-five within three years and have expanded the range and complexity of services offered to them within that time. I have experience of leading teams on high profile acquisition, divestiture and fiscal planning projects. Prior to starting with ABC Co I spent three years working as an accountant for a mid-size firm – XYZ Co. This firm specialised in companies within the technology sector and I gained a strong working knowledge of this sector while working there.
Skills Research what skills and competencies the role requires – and tell them that you have them. You don't need to give STARR-type descriptions of each. It's enough to just mention the skills and competencies. You're basically marking their card and saying 'ask me more about this during the rest of the interview'.	I'm a confident communicator and can explain complex tax concepts with ease and clarity to non-technical clients and to senior management within client companies. I've managed a team of junior associates for the last six years and know how to motivate and bring out the best in team members. Used to working to tight deadlines, I'm resilient and organised and can plan and prioritise multiple tasks and projects.

Education Summarise your qualifications and training and why they are relevant to the role.	I have recently completed a Masters in Management from the Acme School of Business. I also hold a Certificate in Tax Planning for Technology Multinationals from the Institute of Tax and Financial Studies. I completed my accountancy training at CWP Accountancy Firm and qualified as an accountant in 20XX.
Strong Finish Don't fade away. 'What I want to do now is . . .' Make it all about what you can do for them, not what you want for yourself.	I want to use my skills and experience to contribute to the fiscal tax planning of a dynamic company in the technology sector where I can make a real difference to the company's growth and profitability. I strongly believe that I can do that at your company and I would really like to be given the opportunity.

Tell Me About Yourself – template

Work Experience Start with your current role and work back. Mention what you have achieved in your current and previous roles and mention how this is relevant to the job your are interviewing for now.	
Skills Research what skills and competencies the role requires – and tell them that you have them. You don't need to give STARR-type descriptions of each. It's enough to just mention the skills and competencies. You're basically marking their card and saying 'ask me more about this during the rest of the interview'.	

Education Summarise your qualifications and training and why they are relevant to the role.	
Strong Finish Don't fade away. 'What I want to do now is . . .' Make it all about what you can do for them, not what you want for yourself.	

77

What do you know about us? How to do company research

Interviewers need to know that you have really thought about why you want to work there. '*Why did you apply for this role and what do you know about our company?*' '*Because I need a job and your office is close to where I live*' isn't a good answer – and we have heard both. Interviewers won't be impressed that you can recite word perfect the first six lines of the About Us taken from their website's home page. There is no value added or insight in that. Follow our template to figure out what are the five key areas you need to research.

Researching the employer – what do you need to know?

Research Area	Notes
1. Where do they make their money? • Main products/services • Key contributors to sales/profits • Changes in product mix over last three years • Geographical spread of customers	

Research Area	Notes
2. Who are their competitors? • Who are they trying to keep up with/ stay ahead of? • How concentrated are their key markets – lots of competitors or just a few?	
3. Recent Developments • Have they made any significant announcements recently? Have at least two you can mention. • Look on Google News and also on the investor presentations section on their website (if a publicly traded company) for ideas.	
4. Key Challenges • What are the top three challenges/ opportunities for the company for the next two to five years? Is it (for example) competition/regulation/price war/decline of demand for products/cost of investing in technology to stay ahead? Have an opinion on this when they ask you.	
5. The Employees • Do you know anyone who works there now or who has worked there in the past? Use LinkedIn to help you figure that out. • If you know any current or past employees well enough ask them what they like most about working there – this will also help you answer the question 'Why do you want to work here?'	

78

Should you speak to people you know working there as part of your preparation before your interview?

Yes, definitely. And when they ask you in the interview what you know about the company start your answer with, '*As part of my preparation for this interview I spoke to someone/a few people who currently work here and they have told me . . .*' To be honest, it really hardly matters what you say next. The fact that you went to that level of preparation will be hugely impressive to them.

The only time it's not a good idea is if you think that the person you want to speak to may be part of the decision-making process. You don't want your innocent queries to be interpreted as trying to ingratiate yourself to them or get an advantage over other candidates – AKA canvassing. Find another way to get the information you want.

79

Strengths and weaknesses

Seriously? Can't interviewers show a little bit of imagination rather than asking you to talk about your strengths and weaknesses? This question has been around since interviewing began. Unfortunately lots of interviewers still have it on their list of questions and it's usually a go-to question for any interviewers that don't have much experience. Here's how to answer it.

Strengths: Easy. They are whatever the job description says the job requires. Why on earth would you tell them anything different? Use the second section of your Tell Me About Yourself answer – see the guide in 76. Tell them you know what's required and that you have them. A word of warning, however. The first time you say out loud that you are really good at motivating teams and that you have excellent decision-making skills you may feel like you are bragging. You'll think, '*I can't possibly say that to someone. I sound ridiculously full of myself.*' STOP! Resist the temptation to cover your strengths in a veil of false modesty. This is an interview and you need to tell them how good you are. We had a client who we could see was a top-class communicator. When we asked them during an interview training session what their strengths were the first thing they said was, '*People say I'm not too bad at communicating with others.*' Talk about zero impact. Could you have watered it down any more?

Weaknesses: Do NOT say you work too hard or that you are a perfectionist. They won't believe you and they will be disappointed that you reached for the most obvious and overused answer in the whole world. Nul points.

Instead, think of something that is relevant to the role but not a deal-breaker if you tell them you don't have it or need to get better at it. A more useful way to think of Weaknesses is: *What could you **improve on** rather than what are you **absolutely useless** at?* For example, you are applying for a finance role and you have experience of using software packages A and B, but not C. You know that they use B and very occasionally they use C as it is a legacy system. When they ask about what you need to improve on you tell them: '*While I am very used to using software packages A and B I know that you also use C here from time to time. I have not used C before but from what I can tell I think that there are several similarities between the packages. I got myself up to speed really quickly on B and even trained some of my colleagues on how to use it. I'm sure I will be able to pick up what I need to know about C very quickly.*' Job done. Your weakness is now no big deal.

And if you're in the interview and can't think of a single thing you need to improve on tell them that you are not too comfortable giving presentations or speaking in public to a group but that you are working on it. Very few people like doing presentations. The interviewers will be nodding at you in agreement and shared sympathy.

80

Should you look up your interviewer's profile on LinkedIn before the interview?

Yes – and let them know you are doing it.

If they haven't given you the names of your interviewers, email and ask for them. Once you have them don't hide behind LinkedIn's anonymous searching option. You are selling yourself in the interview. You need as much information as possible about who you are selling to. If the interviewer has their profile on LinkedIn it's publicly available information and fair game. We have heard of some companies that actually give extra points in the interview if the candidate looks up the interviewer on LinkedIn before the interview. Know your enemy.

81

How do I get out of work to do an interview – will I pretend to be sick?

Congratulations, you have a face-to-face interview on Tuesday at 1.30 p.m. for a job you would love. But you already have a job and you don't want your boss to know you're thinking of leaving. If your interview is at any time other than first thing in the morning, we recommend you take the day off work. It is really difficult to perform at your best in an interview if you are squeezing it in between the daily demands of your current job, mumbling something about a dental appointment as you make your way out of the office looking better than you have done in months.

What if you have zero holiday days left to take? If you are going to attend the interview you will need to come up with something. Our advice here is to be as vague as possible with your explanation for why you are not at work. Less is definitely more. We have heard of people who recounted in graphic detail the horrors of the bout of food poisoning which kept them off work yesterday – only to resign for a new job two weeks later. It then becomes immediately obvious to everyone that the food poisoning story was a cover for their interview attendance. Why spin so many lies and shred your credibility with colleagues when a vague '*I was feeling under the weather*' or '*I had an appointment*' will suffice?

82

Logistics

You have enough stress going on trying to remember your answers – at least know how to get to the interview.

We've all heard the horror stories. Candidate pitches up ten minutes before the interview to be told that ***as it stated on the invitation email*** (subtext: if you had bothered to read it properly you loser) the interview is actually taking place at the company's other office – a twenty-five-minute drive away. To keep any hope of you being interviewed alive the right thing to do at this point is to call your interviewer or the HR department, apologise and tell them that you will be late. Give them a realistic estimate of when you will get there and ask them if it would be possible to still be interviewed. Sometimes they may be able to rearrange the schedule to accommodate you. It's worth a TRY.

Figuring out where the interview is on and how long it will take you to get there is basic stuff. With all of the uncertainties around interviews this is one thing that is totally within your control. So control the controllables.

And always, always, ALWAYS save a contact number for the interviewer or whoever has set up the interview into your phone. Trying to scroll through emails on your phone to find a contact number once you've realised you will be late is beyond streesful, and probably illegal as you are more than likely driving at the time. Avoid.

83

What to wear

Things have got a lot more complicated than just throwing on the standard dark 'interview suit' – the universal go-to interview gear of old.

There are some industries and roles such as software engineers or developers where if you turned up for the interview wearing a formal suit and shirt/tie they would question straightaway if you were a good fit to the company. You need to use your judgement and wear what you think is appropriate to the role and the environment.

Regardless of the industry you need to look clean, well groomed and as if you made an effort. First impressions matter – a lot. Prior to the interview, take your cue from others who work there, ask around or scour the company website for clues on what people wear to work. Then take your clothing one notch up. While existing employees have earned the right to pitch up to work in slogan t-shirts, shorts and flip-flops you are still on the outside trying to get in. The most unhelpful and undefined of all dress codes – **smart casual** – is best applied when you know you don't have to wear a suit but don't know what you should wear. For men, this usually translates to a collared shirt or t-shirt, chinos or dark jeans, maybe a blazer depending on the role and proper shoes – not trainers. For women – trousers or a skirt with a smart shirt, jumper or cardigan. Go easy on the heels – you should be able to walk confidently into the interview without fear of falling over. Colour is good for all.

Don't fade into the background. If you are the final candidate of the day to be interviewed you will wake them up with your bright appearance and if you were one of the first candidates you will have a better chance of being remembered.

84

I think I can. I know I can. Visualising success

I was recently explaining to someone the importance of being able to **visualise** yourself striding with purpose into the interview room and confidently shaking hands with the interviewer. They looked at me as if I had lost it and said, '*It's just a job interview, Sinéad, not the Olympics.*'

For most of us, a job interview is a big deal so in addition to preparing your answers do whatever you can to give yourself an advantage. Try to get to see the interview room before the interview. This is always easier if you are interviewing with your existing employer for an internal role. Admittedly another employer probably won't agree to let you wander around their building the day before your interview, but at least go to the location of the interview one of the days beforehand. Being familiar with your surroundings – even the outside of the building – will help to reduce your nerves.

Get yourself deep into the self-belief zone. If you can't look in the mirror and tell yourself – out loud – that you will be great in that job then the chances of you convincing the interviewers of that are slim to none. We had a client recently whose first words upon arriving at the office, before they even sat down for their two-hour interview training session were, '*I don't know why I'm even going for this job, I haven't a hope of getting it.*' We suggested that unless they changed their mindset – fast – they would be better off cancelling the training and saving themselves some money.

I think I can.

I know I can.

Say it ten times.

Elite athletes play motivating and empowering music in the hours before a match or a race. Research has consistently shown that playing motivating music improves concentration, confidence and performance when facing a challenging situation. So no, your interview isn't the Olympics, but you should prepare for it like it is.

85

First impressions – formed quickly and difficult to change

Whether they are even aware of it or not, in the first two to three minutes the interviewer meets you they are assessing and forming opinions of you **not** based on what you are saying but on *everything else*. What you wear, how you present yourself, your body language and posture, eye contact, the tone of your voice, the pace of your speech and how you use inflection to emphasise what you are saying. Add to this the fact that people are fundamentally unconsciously biased to favour people who are similar to themselves and biased against those that are different to themselves. All of this means that the point of maximum impact in your interview will be the first few minutes.

Be aware of the powerful effect non-verbal communication has on your interviewer's perception of your ability to do the job. Get your appearance right. Ask someone in the industry for their honest view of what you are planning to wear. Practise a confident entry into the room and the all-important answer to Tell Me About Yourself. First impressions stick – make yours a good one.

86

Shake their hand and take a seat

Unless you are expressly told not to, always initiate a handshake – firm and dry please – when you walk into the interview room. It will make you look in control and confident (even if you're not feeling it). And can we enquire when was the last time you asked someone for permission to sit down when you walked into a room? You never do it when you walk into a meeting room at work but in interviews we seem to become a whole lot less confident about what to do with ourselves. You do not need to hover over the chair waiting for the interviewer to tell you it's okay to sit down. You're not in the principal's office for bad behaviour. Just shake the interviewer's hand and sit down – ready for the first question.

87

Should I bring notes into the interview with me?

The short answer here is no. They are not going to be impressed that you need to refer to notes when answering their questions. Some employers will tell you that you are permitted to bring a copy of your competency-based application form with you into the interview. We would advise that you don't. Furiously flicking through the pages of the application form trying to find your answer to the question they have just asked makes you look totally out of control.

Another client asked us recently if they could write notes when in the interview. They wanted to write down the question they were being asked as the interview went along in case they forgot the question while answering it. Again we would advise against this. If you think you may forget the question when you are halfway through answering it then repeat the question back to them before you start your answer. This will help you to stay on track.

88

Water – Yes
Food – No

Do not take food into the interview. No one wants to watch or hear you eat. And by food we also mean chewing gum. Most interviewers will provide you with some water but often it's in one of those flimsy disposable cups and there is always a slightly terrifying risk that you will hold it too tightly and spill the whole contents all over yourself – or worse – the interviewer. Bring your own water bottle and drink from that if you need to.

89

What the hell are you asking me?

They've asked you a question. You can't figure out how to answer it because you have absolutely no clue what the question even means. They may as well be speaking another language. What are your options? None of the recommended options involve you just saying the first thing that comes into your head and hoping for the best – the 'spray and pray approach'. Not a good plan. What can you do?

You can ask them to repeat the question (and hope that this might ignite a spark of inspiration for you). They say, '*No problem,*' and repeat the question. Unfortunately, that has not helped. You are still in the dark about what they are asking. You can then ask them to rephrase the question. It is perfectly acceptable to say, '*I'm sorry, but I'm not sure I fully understand what you're asking me. Would you mind rephrasing the question?*' That is exactly what you would say if you were in a meeting and someone asked you something you didn't understand. Why should you approach it any differently when you are in an interview? You won't give a good answer if you don't understand what they're asking. Get clarification.

90

Hands up.
I just don't know the answer

All is going well until they ask, '*Of the business risks identified in the Towards 2030 Strategy document, which would you say are the most significant?*' Problem. You haven't read the Towards 2030 Strategy document. In fact, you hadn't even heard about it until right now. Admit defeat here. Don't try to pretend you have read it. They will favour honesty over clumsily chancing your arm. But there are different ways to tell them you don't know. The first (and most definitely not recommended) is to look at them blankly and say, '*I don't know*' or '*I haven't read that.*' If there are ten marks going for that question you've just earned yourself a zero. Try to maintain credibility by saying something like, '*I have done a lot of research for this interview today, but unfortunately my research didn't include this strategy document. However, I could discuss my views on the risks to the business based on the reports I **have** read. Would that be useful?*' It's worth a shot.

91

That was a terrible answer. What can I do?

If you think you can give a better answer then ask for permission to start the answer again. Their time constraints will determine if they will say yes or no but either way it shows that you are self-aware and not afraid to speak up if you think you can improve things – qualities that employers actively seek out. It's worth asking them – but do it at most once or twice per interview. We can't imagine employers would be too accommodating if you wanted to re-do every answer.

92

What are they WRITING?

Interviewers write what you say. They need to take notes to help them reach a decision once they have interviewed all candidates. If you are being interviewed by just one person, rather than a panel, expect that you will spend some of the time talking to the top of their head while they are writing and not looking at you. Don't let it put you off.

93

Do you have any questions for us? How to respond

Firstly, don't put obstacles in the way of them offering you the job by asking questions that make it sound like you may be difficult to deal with. All of the questions you have around flexible working, paid time off to complete training courses or having the opportunity to relocate to the London office after six months can WAIT until you get offered the job. You have leverage when they tell you that they want you. Ask them then.

We recommend you do ask a question even just to demonstrate that you have spent long enough thinking about them to come up with one.

Questions around the structure of the team you will be joining, how many in the team, how does it work with the other teams in the organisation are all worth asking. You will genuinely like to know how the team is structured and it will sound like you have been thinking about how you will fit in.

You can also mention something you have seen in the media about the company and ask how it will impact the organisation. For example: '*I read that you are switching production of the micro product from the Greendale plant to the Whitecliff plant. Do you have any more plans to change what is produced in this plant? Would this have an impact on the type of work the finance department will be doing?'* Again, this demonstrates that you've done your research and you are asking a question to determine the scope and nature of the work you will be doing.

Don't ask them anything that you can get the answer to by just looking on their website for less than ten minutes. A company told us that a candidate asked them in the interview who their main competitors were. They didn't get the job.

If you don't have any questions don't just say a flat, '*No*' when they ask you if you have any. It sounds like you really couldn't be bothered to trouble yourself to think of one. Instead say, '*I've done a lot of research for the interview and have spoken to people working in the company so at this stage I don't have any questions. Thanks.*'

94

How do they score my interview?

Larger organisations and public sector employers will use a structured scoring matrix to assess and compare candidates. Prior to the interview they will identify what the key requirements and competencies are for the role and will then assign a fixed number of marks for each category. While occasionally an employer might tell the candidates what the scoring criteria is in advance of the interview, most employers won't share that information with you before your interview.

As the candidate your aim is very simple: get your scores as high as possible on every category by giving them very strong evidence that you have what they want. The candidate who gets the highest total score gets the job offer. Winner takes all.

Smaller organisations may adopt a much more ad-hoc approach to deciding which candidate is best for the role. The rigour and transparency associated with the structured scoring matrix can go out the window. Everything from: *I just think they will be great* to *We just had better candidates* can be a reason given for justifying choosing or rejecting a candidate.

Sample Candidate Scoring Matrix

Scoring Criteria	Maximum Marks	Candidate Marks
Work Experience – Range	25	
Work Experience – Depth	25	
Innovation	20	
Project Management Organisation & Planning	10	
Leadership	10	
Knowledge of the sector and our company	10	
Totals	**100**	

95

Blindsided

My interview is tomorrow at 9 a.m. I have three hours to prepare.

Divide your time into two equal parts. Spend the first half of your time figuring out 'Why them' and the second half on gathering evidence for 'Why me'.

Why them: Find out where they make their money – what are their products/services and who buys them. Check Google News to see if there have been any significant announcements about them over the last six months. You may be able to use one of them as a reason as to why you want to work there. Look at the job description, pick three of the role's responsibilities/ tasks listed and be ready to tell them that this responsibility/ activity is what is attracting you to the role.

Why me: Pick four of the competencies mentioned in the job description and think of a time when you showed each one. Use STARR to structure your answers and say each of them out loud three times. Practise your opening statement – have three lines on each of your last three roles (reverse chronological order) and tell them that what you've done in the past is very similar to what this role requires. Have an upbeat can-do closing statement that is all about how you want to use your experience, education and skills to contribute to the success of this company and that you know you can make a significant contribution.

96

Is there anything else you would like to add? What's the last thing you say before you leave the room?

By the time they get to asking you this they are starting to think about the next candidate. You've had your time. They do not want a long answer. Keep it to thirty seconds and depart the interview with your confident exit line ringing in their ears. Take a look at what you have used for the Strong Finish section of your Tell Me About Yourself and borrow from that – see 76. Don't allow them to pass you off as the 'easy no' – the person who they can safely reject because they don't think you will care. This may be a risk if you didn't show them that you are sufficiently interested in or determined to get the role.

Try something like this and maintain solid eye contact with them as you say it.

'*Thank you for interviewing me. I would like to finish by saying that I know I have the experience and skills to make a significant contribution to this role and the company. I would really like to be given the opportunity.*'

97

Interview life cycle

This is a typical interview life cycle:

Interview candidate just after the interview: '*That was such an ORDEAL. I'll never forget it as long as I live.*'

Interview candidate a week later when we ask them what questions they were asked: '*Errrr – problem solving, I think? Maybe something about teams? Sorry, can't remember any of the others.*'

By far the most productive interview preparation you can do is to complete an analysis and review of the interview you have just done – even if you get the job. Remember when we said that interviewers are highly predictable? The questions you were asked in your recent interview are highly likely to be very similar to the ones you get asked in the next interview you do. Learn from it.

After the interview, make a note of the questions you were asked and what you said. That's not all, though. It is just as important to document your analysis and reflection of how effective you thought the answer you gave them was – a commentary on your performance. See an example below:

What they asked: *They asked me to tell them about a time when I was involved in a conflict with a colleague and how I dealt with it. I told them the story about the disagreement with ABC re the product launch.*

How did I do? *I think I should have spent more time describing the steps I took to try to minimise the conflict as they kept asking me what else I did. I probably spent too long giving them the technical background on the product and how it works – they didn't seem that interested in that bit. They asked me what I learned from the experience so I should remember to include that if I am asked that question again.*

Trust us – you will be beyond happy with yourself when you start preparing for your next interview and have these notes to work from.

98

And then you go and spoil it all . . . Should you send an email to the interviewer after the interview?

Everything was going so well. You did a great interview. The interviewer was about to email to offer you the job and then they see a lengthy gushing *thank you for interviewing me* email from you in their inbox. The email is full of how wonderful the company is and how it has always been your dream to work there. Next!

If you are going to send a thank you email keep it short and professional – for example:

Dear XXX.

I really enjoyed meeting you on Tuesday and discussing my suitability for the role. Thank you for taking the time to interview me.

Kind regards,

Better still, incorporate your interviewer thank you into an invitation to connect with you on LinkedIn. It's good to say thanks but don't go over the top and scare them off.

99

I've done all my preparation but I'm still NERVOUS AS HELL. What can I do?

Firstly, you would be a robot if you were not experiencing some nerves before you walk into an interview. It's a totally unnatural experience to talk to a stranger for up to forty-five minutes about how wonderful you are. Worse still if you know the interviewer because the role is an internal promotion. Mortifying. You won't eliminate nerves completely, but here are some things you can do to prevent nerves from sabotaging your performance:

- As you walk into the interview, visualise yourself taking a few steps up onto a stage. This is a performance. You are on show and will be saying things that you wouldn't normally say in the course of normal conversation. Get into character and start the performance.
- Do not attempt to learn answers off by heart. Relying on your memory to recall the exact words in the exact order is a bad strategy. You are putting yourself under too much pressure. Use your Trigger Words and tell your story in your own words.
- Stand up while you are waiting outside the interview room. Most candidates sit hunched on a chair, arms

folded, head down. It's as if they are trying to disappear. Make yourself as big as you can. Try some power posing (although you may have to retreat to the bathroom in case people around you think you've lost it). Research[1] has shown that by commanding a powerful stance for just two minutes we can make ourselves feel more powerful and more confident when facing a high stress situation such as an interview. Do it.

• Get used to **Pause and Repeat.** When you are asked a question, pause for two seconds, repeat the question back to them and **then** start to answer it. This will avoid you blurting out the first (sometimes random) thing that comes into your nervous head.

---

[1] 'P-Curving a More Comprehensive Body of Research on Postural Feedback Reveals Clear Evidential Value for Power-Posing Effects: Reply to Simmons and Simonsohn' (2017), *Psychological Science*, 2018, Vol. 29(4) 656–666, Amy J. C. Cuddy, S. Jack Schultz, Nathan E. Fosse

If at first you don't succeed . . .
Get feedback

You really wanted this job. You thought you did a good enough interview. Maybe you could have answered one or two of the questions a little better? The email arrives.

Dear XXXX, Thank you for interviewing for the role of Purchasing Manager in our Electronics division. Unfortunately . . .

You don't need to read any more. Gutted. Chances are you probably feel like putting it out of your mind and trying to forget about it. However, you will be far more likely to do a better interview next time if you ask for feedback on the ones you didn't get. As hard as it is to hear, you may learn something that you can fix for next time. Rather than going on the defensive and asking, '*WHY didn't I get the job?*' switch the request to, '*I was really disappointed I didn't get this job. It would be great if there was any specific feedback you could give me so that I can work on it for my next interview.*' You may feel uncomfortable asking it but it will be worth it when you get the advice.

Although you've asked them for feedback, some companies will just completely ignore you and you will never get any more from them than the thanks-but-no-thanks letter. But it's always worth asking.

And finally – let's talk about money.
What are your salary expectations?

Be ready to answer this question. Do your homework. When you tell them what you are expecting, be able to justify where the number is coming from. Wishful thinking, plucking a number from thin air or 'because I'm worth it' are not good sources.

Consult the salary surveys produced each year by the larger recruitment consultant firms and see where the market is for this type of role and your experience.

Consider if you have additional experience or skills that will add more value to the company and for which they may pay over the market rate.

Remuneration is more than just the stated salary. A generous benefits package including pension contributions, healthcare, commission, holidays, flexible working and other employee provisions should be given a monetary value by you and added to the salary number when comparing different offerings.

Give them a range when telling them what salary you are targeting. For example, if you are looking to earn €60,000 tell them that you are targeting a salary in the €60,000–€65,000 range. Put your target at the end of the range you quote them. Always add that you will review the entire salary and benefits package as you know that there can be significant value in the benefits.